FAITH OF OUR FOUNDING FATHERS

Leo Godzich

Published by NAME
The National Association of Marriage Enhancement

For more information and additional resources contact:
www.nameonline.net
or
NAME National Headquarters
P. O. Box 30777
Phoenix, Arizona
85046-0777

602-404-2600
602-971-7127 fax
info@nameonline.net

Unless otherwise indicated, all Scriptures quotations are taken from the New King James version of the Bible. Copyright © 1979, 1980, 1982 by Thomas Nelson, Inc. Used by permission. All rights reserved.

Scripture quotations marked KJV are from the King James Version.

Credit for Cover Design:
The vision of *Liberty for All* was laid on my heart five weeks before 9-11. My prayer is that it will reach the nations in spirit and truth, ministering for Christ the true meaning of freedom.   *Garrett Walker*
Email: compcomstudios@aol.com   Phone: 602.577.6904

Library of Congress Cataloging-in-Publication Data:
Godzich, Leo M.
   Faith of Our Founding Fathers / Leo Godzich
ISBN 0-9712847-2-5
1. American History - Christian 2. Godzich, Leo

Printed in the United States of America

Dedication

To my mother, Anna Godzich, in loving memory of my father, Kazimierz Godzich, whose boyhood dream of coming to the land of the free was realized, and became one of the greatest blessings in the life of his five sons. His life embodied the characteristics that are outlined in this book. He was my modern-day American hero founding Father.

Leo Godzich
Summary Biography

Leo Godzich is the founder and president of NAME (The National Association of Marriage Enhancement) and the host of the International Marriage Conference as well as chairman of the Covenant Marriage Movement. NAME is a network of churches and couples committed to biblical marriage ministry. NAME is presently developing counseling centers in the U.S., Canada, Africa and Australia, Europe and Asia. Leo is *Pastor of Special Projects* at Phoenix First Assembly of God (Tommy Barnett, Pastor) in Phoenix, Arizona.

Leo and his wife, Molly, oversee a local marriage outreach to hundreds of couples with outstanding results in putting broken marriages back together and building strong marriages. Leo and Molly conduct *Together Forever* Marriage Seminars at churches and hotels around the country. Leo is the author of, *Is God In Your Marriage?*, *Public Relations and the Church* and *Mighty Men: A 50-day Intensive Leadership Development Course*. He has appeared as a guest and host on national television programs.

He founded the Deacon and Deaconess Ministry (altar workers, follow-up, visitation and care) of Phoenix First Assembly. He currently co-ordinates special events and projects at Phoenix First Assembly, the sixth largest church in America of any denomination, according to *Time Magazine*. Leo has organized special events such as "Feed the Multitude" which CNN called "perhaps the largest sit-down dinner in America." At this event an estimated 20,000 people received a full Thanksgiving dinner, prepared and served entirely by volunteers. He was the organizer of World Prayer Meeting USA; a satellite joined simultaneous prayer meeting originating from Phoenix and Seoul, Korea in which an estimated 12 million people participated in prayer for worldwide revival in October of 1994.

He pioneered ministry to people with AIDS and is the founder and director of LAMP Ministries, an outreach program to HIV positive people and their families.

Leo has preached in various cities across the nation and around the world. A popular speaker, Leo has spoken to national meetings such as SmartMarriages, PromiseKeepers, National Street Ministries Conference, the Dunamis Conference, Church Growth Festival, Pastors' and Leaders' School and others.

Prior to entering the ministry, Leo had been in a variety of different business endeavors and is an accomplished writer. Formerly an award-winning journalist, he has had more than 300 articles published in various publications and as editor-in-chief of Jersey Business Review was the youngest editor of a statewide business publication in America. Pastor Leo Godzich, his wife, Molly, and daughters, Emily, Bethany and Christy live in Phoenix, Arizona.

A pioneer in social reform legislation Leo was the chief proponent of Covenant Marriage License Law and the Marriage Skills and Communication Bill, and has testified before legislative bodies numerous times.

Faith of Our Founding Fathers

Introduction..7

The American Experiment: A Faith-Based Initiative..................9

The Pursuit of Happiness: A Political Community..................29

True Justice: A Common Higher Authority..............................47

Unwavering Courage: A Sacred Honor....................................73

The Success of Industry: Work Improves Everybody's Life.........89

The Learned Life: Inspired Understanding............................101

Faith of Our Founding Fathers: Opportunity for Revival..........117

Introduction

This book is not a narrative, nor is it history, nor is it a lengthy social commentary. What then is this book and why is it relevant for me? You may ask.

I purposefully resisted the temptation to include more of my personal thoughts and observations upon the materials contained herein. Rather, I prefer to view this book as a compendium of thought -- -- not modern-day analysis, and certainly not commentary on the founding fathers. Instead, it is my hope that you, dear reader, would be pulled in by the series of fascinating quotations arranged in a manner to hopefully help you draw the conclusions that seem so apparent.

It is my humble opinion that we have lost sight of the vision of our founding fathers, and we have only done so relatively recently. I love America and it is my desire that this look at the founding fathers through their own words would help others who perhaps have not had the opportunity to experience life in other countries to love America from the bottom of their heart.

When my father was a little boy in Poland, he heard people speak of the country in which immigrants with almost nothing to begin with could experience immediate opportunity to rapidly advance their living conditions while enjoying the most widespread freedoms on the face of the earth. At that point in the early 20th-century, a little Polish boy determined in his heart that someday he would not only see that country but would also take advantage of the opportunity for freedom.

It took him five decades of adventurous living, which included more than four years as a prisoner in Nazi Germany, the loss of his only daughter to disease, and banishment by the threat of losing life itself from his native Poland because of his political perspective prior to Communist takeover, and other adventures.

In February 1962, Kazimierz Godzich, his wife Anna and their five sons arrived in New York City in fulfillment of a little boy's dream.

He worked several jobs and odd jobs at the same time in order to provide for his family and to create educational and lifestyle opportunities so that his children could take advantage of his American dream. Among the accomplishments of his five sons (some of them occurring after his passing away) are the following:

Positions held in diverse professions and locations such as State Department interpreters, authors and advocates of legislation, professorships at leading universities, top-level executive positions at multinational corporations, political consultancies including a job in the White House and in presidential election campaigns, public speaking engagements before audiences numbering in the thousands, authorship of books, pioneering efforts on the Internet including the test case of free speech on the World Wide Web, major group travel organizing, radio talk show host, sports coach, international philanthropic and charitable efforts, and much more.

And that's all about my brothers! I will not add my accomplishments to the list, because my biography, with some achievements, is listed elsewhere in this book.

The point I'm making is that a little Polish boy had a dream of taking advantage of the American experiment of freedom, believing that his generations would have a positive impact on their families, communities, the nation and the world -- -- much the same way that America's founding fathers believed that the expression of freedom founded in self-government and rooted in Christian tradition, presented the greatest opportunity for achievement and service to fellow men.

I will never forget the day, some seven years after we had come to this country, when we accompanied my father to the U.S. Immigration and Naturalization Service office where, with tears in his eyes, he placed his hand on his heart and in his broken English recited the Pledge of Allegiance to the United States of America as he was sworn in as a naturalized U.S. citizen.

It bothers me when those who have benefited all their lives from the political ideology of America so casually take for granted our freedoms and how they came to be. This book is a humble attempt to help some Americans enjoy a greater understanding of how their roots have blessed the entire world.

As William Bennett put it, "though the founders set standards that many of us, most of us, cannot hope to meet, their thoughts on patriotism and national greatness, on the proper relationship between God and men, men and women, work and leisure, and friends and strangers might help us to do better."

Dear reader, open your heart and experience the thoughtfulness, wisdom, passion and perseverance of our founding fathers and the guiding principles of their faith.

The American Experiment:
A Faith-Based Initiative

As these United States were being formed European onlookers wondered whether the American experiment would last the test of time from its tumultuous beginnings. Never before in the history of mankind had a government been founded on the principles that each man should have the right for freedom of worship.

Most Americans today do not realize that this foundational right was a core value for our founding fathers. In fact, many believe that the notion of **"a government of the people, by the people and for the people"** was established as a result of the cumulative genius of our founding fathers. History books today ignore the fact that this concept was indeed a biblical concept that had been advocated four centuries earlier as an explanation of how the Holy Bible should be used to establish a government that would be a blessing to its people.

In the late 14th century, an Oxford University professor named John Wycliffe changed the nature of religion and philosophical thought when he successfully became the first to translate the entire Bible from the Latin Vulgate into English. This single act was a foundation for religious reformers who, as a result of Wycliffe's work, then recognized that the written Scriptures should be available for the common man.

This development in and of itself was viewed as a threat to the monarchy of England as it related to the government's ability to control matters of religion as well as impose them upon its people. In a sense, Wycliffe's translation of the Bible into English really laid the groundwork for those who later would envision that a greater form of government should be available to people of faith.

It was in 1384 that John Wycliffe, in the prologue of his English Bible, declared that the Holy Scriptures illuminated a godly purpose in the governmental affairs of men:

The Bible is for the Government of the People, by the People, and for the People.[1]

The founding fathers of the United States of America indeed embraced this principle as a fundamental ideal in the establishment of this new nation dedicated to keeping its people free from tyrannical despotism.

America was a Faith-based initiative.

People of profound faith willing not only to risk their lives but to dedicate their lives and risk their sacred honor, recognized and agreed that biblical principles and a reliance on the providence of their creator would be the only way that this experiment in democracy, the founding of this great republic, could possibly succeed.

Many American schoolchildren today never get the opportunity to understand the faith-based initiative that encouraged all 56 signers of the Declaration of Independence to risk all for the cause of freedom. Ask yourself: do I recall my grade school teacher talking about faith in God as a consistent theme in our Declaration of Independence?

The very last line of the Declaration of Independence leaves no doubt as to where the founding fathers gained their resolve:
"And for the support of this declaration, *with a firm reliance on the protection of Divine Providence*, we mutually pledge to each other our Lives, our Fortunes, and are sacred Honor."

They understood the risk. John Hancock, whose name has become a euphemism for a strong signature because of his large signature as the first signer of the Declaration of Independence, reportedly said, "There! His Majesty can now read my name without glasses. And he can double the reward on my head!"

The faith of men like John Hancock shone through in their comments and writings, as when Hancock said, **"the Lord gave this country and name and the standing among the nations of the world...I hope in prayer that the gratitude of their hearts may be expressed by proper use of those inestimable blessings, by the greatest exertions of patriotism, by forming and supporting institutions for cultivating the human understanding and for the greatest progress of the arts and sciences, by establishing laws for the support of piety, religion, and morality...and by exhibiting on the great theater of the world those social, public and private virtues which give more dignity to a people, possessing their own sovereignty then the crowns and diadems afford to sovereign princes."**[2]

The increasing secularization of our nation, particularly as it applies to primary education, and for that matter secondary education, has kept many of today's Americans in the dark about the faith of our founding fathers. It is important to note that strong religious convictions were the basis of the founding of colonies that would then unite to separate themselves from what was viewed as religious tyranny in England.

In fact, the Pilgrims and the Puritans, known as the early settlers, were most commonly referred to as separatists for their desire to separate themselves from an imposed state religion and to freely worship the God of the Bible as they saw fit.

When Virginia (as the first Colony to receive a charter granted by King James I) organized, its first permanent settlement was known as the Jamestown Colony in 1606. This occurred some 20 years after a settlement had been attempted on Roanoke Island where, in fact, an American Indian named Manteo was the first to be baptized into the Christian faith in America. The Roanoke Colony had suffered disease and death and was disbanded, therefore it was not recognized as a permanent settlement.[3]

Clearly the intent of the founding fathers of this Colony was to propagate the gospel of the Lord Jesus Christ.

On April 10, 1606, the First Charter of Virginia stated:

We, greatly commending and graciously accepting of their Desires for the Furtherance of so noble a Work, which may, by the Providence of Almighty God, hereafter tend to the Glory of His Divine Majesty, in propagating of Christian Religion to such People, as yet live in Darkness and miserable Ignorance of the true Knowledge and Worship of God, and may in time bring the Infidels and Savages, living in those Parts, to human Civility, and to a settled and quiet Government.[4]

Less than three weeks later, another group's initial act after landing at Cape Henry, April 27, 1607, was to erect a wooden cross and commence a prayer meeting, led by the Reverend Robert Hunt. Later that year, after Reverend Hunt's death, the settlers stated:

1607. To the glory of God and in memory of the Reverend Robert Hunt, Presbyter, appointed by the Church of England. Minister of the Colony
which established the English Church and English Civilization at Jamestown, Virginia, in 1607.
His people, members of the Colony, left this testimony concerning him. He was an honest, religious and courageous Divine.
He preferred the Service of God in so good a voyage to every thought of ease at home. He endured every privation, yet none ever heard him repine. During his life our factions were ofte healed, and our greatest extremities so comforted that they seemed easy in comparison with what we endured after his memorable death.
We all received from him the Holy Communion together, as a pledge of reconciliation, for we all loved him for his exceeding goodness. He planted
The first Protestant Church in America and laid down his life in the foundation of America.[5]

Somewhat reminiscent of the New Testament house churches, a separatist named William Brewster in England opened his home as a church in defiance of the Church of England, permitting separatists to meet for worship at his home in Scrooby, England. After persecution, he fled to Holland in 1608.

Governor William Bradford gave account of William Brewster's influence on the Separatist movement from its early beginnings:

"Mr. Brewster went and lived in the country...till the Lord revealed Himself further to him. In the end, the tyranny of the bishops against godly preachers and people, in silencing the former and persecuting the latter, caused him and many more to look further into things, and to realize the unlawfulness of their episcopal callings, and to feel the burden of their many antichristian corruptions, which both he and they endeavoured to throw off....

After they had joined themselves together in communion, as was mentioned earlier, he was a special help and support to them. On the Lord's day they generally met at his house, which was a manor of the bishop's, and he entertained them with great kindness when they came, providing for them at heavy expense to himself. He was the leader of those who were captured at Boston in Lincolnshire, suffering the greatest loss, and was one of the seven who were kept longest in prison and afterwards bound over to the assizes.

He labored in the fields as long as he was able; yet when the church had no other minister he taught twice every Sabbath, and that both powerfully and profitably, to the great edification and comfort of his hearers, many being brought to God by his ministry."[6]

In 1608, after the agreement to separate from the church of England, the Separatists of the Scrooby congregation covenanted together to form a church: **"They shook off the yoke of antichristian bondage, and as ye Lord's free people, joyned themselves (by a covenant of the Lord) into a church estate, in ye fellowship of ye Gospel, to walke in all his wayes, made known or to be made known unto them, according to their best endeavours, whatsoever it should cost them, the Lord assisting them."**[7]

On December 15, 1617, William Brewster and the congregation's pastor, John Robinson, wrote a letter from Leyden, Holland, to Sir Edwin Sandys, a London financier, in which they explained the Separatists' situation and plans:

Knit together as a body in most strict and sacred bond and covenant of the Lord, of the violation whereof we make great conscience, and by virtue whereof we so hold ourselves straitly tied to all care of each other's good, and of the whole by everyone and so mutually.[8]

This was an underlying theme for many of the early settlers: the sense of community and mutual responsibility founded in a "**sacred bond**" and "**covenant of the Lord.**" The Lord referred to is contextually clear as the Lord Jesus Christ, not an obscure reference to a term of British nobility as some secularists would attempt to errantly explain away.

Faith in not just a god, but God in Christian terms, was a foundation upon which notions of liberty in a democratic (note small "d"—not partisan party-related) society could exist. Apart from moral values based on like faith, the American experiment would not have the common ground of that "sacred bond" of mutual responsibility to the community as a whole. Besides, those that had risked life and limb and watched love ones perish during and after the arduous journey to get to the land of religious freedom could scarcely conceive that members of their community would not understand that the only way such a society could survive would be to have a mutual moral code and a covenant with God to uphold such a faith-based moral structure.

Brewster was to become one of the most unsung heroes in American history as he literally became one of the signers of the Mayflower compact after sailing with the Pilgrims on the Mayflower, after which he became one of the most influential leaders of the Plymouth Colony.

In 1629, when a church was founded at Salem in the Massachusetts Bay Colony, William Brewster made this comment:

The church that had been brought over the ocean now saw another church, the first-born in America, holding the same faith in the same simplicity of self-government under Christ alone.[9]

We ought to take special note of the premise of this pioneering statesman of democratic ideals, especially the final phrase: "the same simplicity of self-government under Christ alone." This broke previous notions of government that called for people to be ruled by an authority, such as a king. Brewster understood that self-government required the high moral standard of Christ-likeness in stark contrast to religiosity, which would inevitably establish just another man-made hierarchy.

Brewster carefully chose his words when saying "under Christ alone." "Under" implied willful submission to the authority of Jesus Christ only. Thus Brewster's basis for the simplicity of self-government—in other words complex rule of law is not necessary for a community willfully submitted to the dictates of the Lord Jesus Christ. No earthly dictator was necessary to confine and restrain a people who were already constrained by the principles of their heavenly leader.

In fact, what today has been conveniently secularized as "the golden rule" (doing unto others as you would have them do unto you), was a given in this community of faith as a mutually submitted to code of conduct called for by the

Lord Jesus Christ in the gospel of Matthew, chapter 7 and verse 12: **"Therefore, whatever you want men to do to you, do also to them, for this is the Law and the Prophets."**

In the same manner, other early colonists had a profound sense of Christian covenant, a concept that many Christians don't understand today, much less adhere to. The early settlers revered the opportunity of free worship and the development of a system of self-government as a holy trust imparted from and entered into with God. Covenant was understood as a promise made before, and with, God. Covenant was a vital part of everyday living; a consciousness of the sacred bond, or holy trust, of God was pervasive.

Peter Bulkeley was the Puritan leader who established the city of Concord, Massachusetts in 1636. In his only publication, The Gospel Covenant; or the Covenant of Grace Opened, published in London ten years later, Peter Bulkeley stated:

We are as a city set upon a hill, in the open view of all the earth...We profess ourselves to be a people in covenant with God, and therefore...the Lord our God...will cry shame upon us if we walk contrary to the covenant which we have promised to walk in. If we open the mouths of men against our profession, by reason of the scandalousness of our lives, we (of all men) shall have the greater sin. [10]

Bulkeley's strong words are ones that politicians might do well to have as their light of reflection and self-examination. Indeed, they are cause for pause and reflection for every American. The colonists sensed that the unique opportunity in man's history, that became America, was directly related to the people of a democratic Christian nation walking out their faith because the whole world would watch.

The American attempt at self-government had to be set against the backdrop of Christian moral living if covenant with God was to be upheld. Shame awaited its opportunity to ridicule the notion that people could actually rule themselves by a consensus of like-mindedness. Bulkeley wanted America to show forth the wisdom of God through the practical application of biblical principles of governmental service to the people.

Let us study so to walk that this may be our excellency and dignity among the nations of the world among which we live; that they may be constrained to say of us, only this people is wise, and a holy and blessed people; that all that see us may see and know that the name of the Lord is called upon us; and that we are the seed which the Lord hath blessed. (Deut. 28:10; Isa. 61:9) [11]

The references that Bulkeley included presupposed his readers recognized the authority of the Bible and gave him basis in truth for his observation. To understand the depth of conviction accompanying his statement, one ought include the text of the references:

"Then all peoples of the earth shall see that you are called by the name of the Lord, and they shall be afraid of you." Deuteronomy 28:10 and,

"Their descendants shall be known among the Gentiles, and their offspring among the people. All who see them shall acknowledge them, that they are the posterity whom the Lord has blessed." Isaiah 61:9

The Pilgrims and the Puritans viewed their opportunity for self-government as a blessing that others did not enjoy around the world, and the proper response was to not only honor that, but to maximize its impact so that others would be won over to this way of thought.

In many respects, immigrants to America have always held to this view that there is something greater about America than just opportunity, that indeed, we are to individually do our best so that we could collectively do our best, and be the harbinger of democratic government for others to see and emulate.

Right from the start, both the immigrant populous and the first government officials operated with this sense of political destiny and global vision wrapped up in a spiritual mission.

Governor William Bradford was a Pilgrim leader who helped establish the Plymouth Colony. Sailing in the Mayflower, he was chosen as governor of the colony in 1621, and was re-elected 30 times until his death. In 1650, William Bradford wrote a history of Plymouth Plantation, which is comparable to Shakespeare's works in literary and historical significance. In it, he traced the events that led to the Pilgrims' departure from England:

It is well knowne unto ye godly and judicious how since ye first breaking out of ye lighte of ye gospell in our Honourable Nation of England, (which was ye first of nations whom ye Lord adorned ther with, after the grosse darkness...which had covered and overspread ye Christian world), what warrs and opposissions ever since, Satan, hath raised, maintained, and continued against the Saints, from time to time, in one sort or other.

Some times by bloody death and cruell torments; other whiles imprisonments, banishments, and other hard usages; as being loath his kingdom should goe downe, and trueth prevaile, and ye churches of God reverte to their anciente puritie and recover their primative order, libertie, and bewtie.

But when he could not prevaile by these means againste the maine trueths of ye gospell, but that they began to take rootting in many places, being watered by ye blooud of ye martires, and blessed from heaven with a gracious encrease; he then begane to take him to his anciente strategeme used of old against the first Christians.

That when by ye bloody and barbarous persecutions of ye heathen Emperours, he could not stop and subvert the course of ye gospell, but that it speedily overspred with a wonderfull celeritie the then best known parts...ye professours themselves, (working upon their pride and ambition, with other corrupte passions incident to all mortall men, yea to ye saints themselves in some measure), by which woefull effects followed; as not only bitter contentions, and hartburnings, schismes, with other horrible confusions, but Satan tooke occasion and advantage therby to foyst in a number of vile...cannons and decrees, which have since been as snares to many poore and peacable souls even to this day.

So as in ye anciente times, the persecutions by ye heathen and their Emperours, was not greater than of the Christians one against another.[12]

This statement rang strongly true for our founding fathers when they established the First Amendment to provide for religious liberty. The idea of a country free from a state-imposed form of Christianity meant that the government would not tell people how to worship God. Liberal interpretations devoid of this historical view indicate that separation of church and state was designed to keep the influence of the church out of government, when in fact the contrary was true.

The influence of Christianity permeated nearly everything in government because of the sense of spiritual destiny in the American experiment. The First amendment was indeed designed to assure that no specific "brand" of Christianity, especially one imposed by a religious hierarchy tied into a political aristocracy, would instruct people in matters of doctrine with the weight and authority of government behind it.

In the last several decades, we have seen the interpretation of the First Amendment devoid of this historical perspective used to tell churches and religious organizations what they may or may not do in realms ranging from physical property (zoning laws, etc.) to organizational practices (tax code structure, hiring practices, etc.). This was never the intent of those who recognized God's hand upon this nation. They believed that men were free inasmuch as their ability to worship God was free from the dictates of authoritarian government, but was established on representative government that would not meddle in matters of religious conscience.

This faith-based perspective existed even prior to the actual establishment of the colony at Plymouth.

On November 11, 1620, before setting foot on dry land, Governor William Bradford and the leaders on the Mayflower signed the Mayflower Compact, the first constitutional document of America:

In ye name of God, Amen. We whose names are underwriten, the loyall subjects of our dread soveraigne Lord, King James, by ye grace of God, of Great Britaine, France, & Ireland king, defender of ye faith, etc., having undertaken, for ye glorie of God, and advancemente of ye Christian faith, and honour of our king & countrie, a voyage to plant ye first colonie in ye Northerne parts of Virginia, doe by these presents solemnly & mutually in ye presence of God, and one of another, covenant & combine our selves togeather into a civill body politick, for our better ordering & preservation & furtherance of ye ends aforesaid; and by vertue hearof to enacte, constitute, and frame such just & equall lawes, ordinances, acts, constitutions & offices, from time to time, as shall be thought most meete & convenient for ye generall good of ye Colonie, unto which we promise all due submission and obedience.

In witnes wherof we have hereunder subscribed our names at Cap-Codd ye 11. of November, in ye year of ye raigne of our soveraigne lord,

King James, of England, France, & Ireland ye eighteenth, and by Scotland ye fiftie fourth. Ano:Dom. 1620. [13]

On the very next day, November 12, 1620, the first full day in the New World, Governor William Bradford described the Pilgrims' thankfulness:

Being thus arrived in a good harbor, and brought safe to land, they fell upon their knees and blessed the God of Heaven who had brought them over the vast and furious ocean, and delivered them from all the perils and miseries thereof, again to set their feet on the firm and stable earth, their proper element.[14]

If anyone doubted how biblically based Governor Bradford's world view really was, he need only examine the following statement made at the time of landing and on the day of the Mayflower Compact signing:

What could now sustaine them but ye spirite of God and His grace? May not and ought not the children of these fathers rightly say: Our fathers were Englishmen which came over this great ocean, and were ready to perish in this

wilderness; (Deuteronomy 26:5,7) but they cried unto ye Lord, and He heard their voyce, and looked on their adversitie, etc.

Let them therefore praise ye Lord, because He is good, and His mercies endure for ever. (107 Psalm: v. 1,2,4,5,8) Yea let them which have been redeemed of ye Lord, show how He hath delivered them from ye hand of ye oppressour.

When they wandered in ye deserte wilderness out of ye way, and found no citie to dwell in, both hungrie, and thirstie, their sowle was overwhelmed in them. Let them confess before ye Lord His loving kindness, and His wonderful works before ye sons of men.[15]

This pronouncement that the means of sustenance for these settlers was the Spirit and grace of God is credited as the initial passage that would refer to those settlers as Pilgrims.[16] I daresay that most schoolchildren in the public education system today would not equate the term "pilgrim" with its meaning of a passionately spiritual person on a holy mission to a holy place. Instead, "pilgrim" is usually pictured as a distinctive of wardrobe (funny hat and weird buckled shoes) by schoolchildren.

But the notion of God's ordination of what began at Plymouth was no trivial matter for those pilgrims. Bradford's sense of God's providence is vivid in his understanding of the long term and socio-political implications of those humble beginnings and how the struggle for survival gave God glory as that settlement gave hope for persevering self-government in an environment of freedom to worship. Consider the profundity of his observations 30 years later:

Thus out of small beginnings greater things have been produced by His hand that made all things of nothing, and gives being to all things that are; and, as

one small candle may light a thousand, so the light here kindled hath shone unto many, yea in some sort to our whole nation; let the glorious name of Jehovah have all the praise.[17]

The Mayflower Compact and the History of Plymouth Plantation are two documents that deeply affected the views of many of the signers of our Declaration of Independence, and of many early Americans who admired Bradford's leadership and pioneering efforts. The testimony of his ability to see future implications, and of his strong faith, is found upon his tombstone. At Burial Hill, Plymouth, Massachusetts, Governor William Bradford's grave is inscribed:

Under this stone rests the ashes of William Bradford, a zealous Puritan, and sincere Christian Governor of Plymouth Colony from 1621 to 1657, aged 69, except 5 years, which he declined. "Let the right hand of the Lord awake." [Hebrew] "What our fathers with so much difficulty attained do not basely relinquish."[Latin]

Perhaps the heartcry of this book is best summed up in the final line of his tombstone: "What our fathers with so much difficulty attained do not basely relinquish." Many would argue that it is too late, that we have already basely relinquished what the founding fathers stood for.

However, I don't think that is true. For the most part, we have strayed from the original intent of the settlers of winning people to Jesus Christ, of relying on God and of the Bible as our presiding moral code. But there is a remnant of people that believe we can revive this nation toward its original state of blessing.

The province of New Jersey, on its seal in 1697, chose to inscribe the Bible verse that most adequately expresses that hope:

Righteousness exalteth a nation. Proverbs 14:34 [18]

John Adams is viewed by many as the chief architect of the Declaration of Independence. He handed the pen to Thomas Jefferson to write it, knowing his limitations in popularity with some of the factions could be a hindrance to ratification of the revolutionary document. In his "Dissertation on the Canon and Feudal Law" in 1765, Adams stirred the colonists to not forget their heritage of the settlers before them as they battled for their rights and freedoms in the present day. We should take notice in the same manner today, and not relinquish the memory of our spiritual heritage as a people:

Let us read, recollect and impress upon our souls the views and ends of our own more immediate forefathers, in exchanging their native country for a dreary, inhospitable wilderness. Let's examine the nature of that power and the cruelty of that oppression, which drove them from their homes. Recollect their amazing fortitude, their bitter sufferings, the hunger, the nakedness and the cold, which they patiently endured -- -- the severe labors of clearing the grounds, building their houses and raising their provisions, amidst dangerous wild beasts and savage men, before they had time, money or materials for commerce. Recollect the civil and religious principles, hopes and expectations, which constantly supported and carried them through all hardships with patience and resignation. We must recollect it was liberty, the hope of liberty for themselves and for us and ours, which conquered all discouragements, dangers and trials. In such researches as this, let us all in our several departments cheerfully engage -- -- but especially the proper patrons and supporters of law, learning and religion!

Let the pulpits resound with the doctrines and sentiments of religious liberty. Let us hear the danger of thralldom to our consciences from ignorance, extreme poverty, and dependence, in short, from civil and political slavery. Let us see delineated before us the true map of man. Let us hear the dignity of his nature, and the noble rank he holds among the works of God -- -- that consenting to slavery is a sacrilegious breach of trust, as offensive in the sight of God as it is derogatory from our own honor or interest or happiness -- -- and then God Almighty has promulgated from heaven liberty, peace and goodwill to man![19]

---

[1] Wycliffe, John. General Prologue of the Wycliffe Translation of the Bible, 1384. John Bartlett, Bartlett's Familiar Quotations (Boston: Little, Brown and Company, 1863, 1955), p. 1021.

[2] John Hancock's life and speeches: a personalized vision of the American Revolution, editor Paul D. Brands, page 332, Speech in Council Chamber, February 27,1788

[3] The World Book Encyclopedia, 18 vols. (Chicago, IL: Field Enterprises, Inc., 1957; W.F. Quarrie and Company, 8 vols., 1917; World Book, Inc., 22 vols., 1989), Vol. 12, p. 5732; Vol. 10, p. 4596.

[4] Virginia, First Charter of. 1606, granted by King James I. Ebenezer Hazard, editor, Historical Collections: Consisting of State Papers and other Authentic Documents; Intended as Materials for an History of the United States of America (Philadelphia: T. Dobson, 1792), Vol. I, pp. 50-51.

[5] Inscription of original 1607 Settler's testimony engraved upon the bronze Robert Hunt Memorial, Jamestown Island, Virginia.

[6] Brewster, William. 1644, as described in William Bradford (Governor of Plymouth Colony), The History of Plymouth Plantation 1608-1650 (Boston, Massachusetts: Massachusetts Historical Society, 1856; Boston, Massachusetts: Wright and Potter Printing Company, 1898, from the original manuscript; rendered in Modern English, Harold Paget, 1909; NY: Russell and Russell, 1968; San Antonio, TX: American Heritage Classics, Mantle Ministries, 228 Still Ridge, Bulverde, Texas, 1988), pp. 314-319.

[7] Verna M. Hall, The Christian History of the Constitution of the United States of America - Christian Self-Government with Union (San Francisco: Foundation for American Christian Education, 1976), p. 185. Marshall Foster and Mary-Elaine Swanson, The American Covenant - The Untold Story (Roseburg, OR: Foundation for Christian Self-Government, 1981; Thousand Oaks, CA: The Mayflower Institute, 1983, 1992), p. 69.

[8] Brewster, William. December 15, 1617, in a letter written from William Brewster and the congregation's pastor, John Robinson, from Leyden (Holland) to Edwin Sandys, a London financier. William Bradford (Governor of Plymouth Colony), The History of Plymouth Plantation 1608-1650 (Boston, Massachusetts: Massachusetts Historical Society, 1856; Boston, Massachusetts: Wright and Potter Printing Company, 1898, 1901, from the Original Manuscript, Library of Congress Rare Book Collection, Washington, D.C.; rendered in Modern English, Harold Paget, 1909; NY: Russell and Russell, 1968; NY: Random House, Inc., Modern Library College edition, 1981; San Antonio, TX: American Heritage Classics, Mantle Ministries, 228 Still Ridge, Bulverde, Texas, 1988), pp. 34-35.

[9] Brewster, William. 1629, comment after a church was founded in the Massachusetts Bay Colony. Leonard Bacon, The Genesis of the New England Church (New York: Harper and Brothers, Publishers, 1874), p. 475. Marshall Foster and Mary-Elaine Swanson, The American Covenant - The Untold Story (Roseburg, OR: Foundation for Christian Self-Government, 1981; Thousand Oaks, CA: The Mayflower Institute, 1983, 1992), pp. 88-89.

[10] Bulkeley, Peter. 1651. The Gospel Covenant; or the Covenant of Grace Opened (London: 2nd edition, 1651), pp. 431-32. The Annals of America, 20 vols. (Chicago, IL: Encyclopedia Britannica, 1968), Vol. I, pp. 212-221.

[11] Bulkeley, Peter. 1651. The Gospel Covenant; or the Covenant of Grace Opened (London: 2nd edition, 1651), pp. 431-32. The Annals of America, 20 vols. (Chicago, IL: Encyclopedia Britannica, 1968), Vol. I, p. 212.

[12] Bradford, William. 1650, The History of Plymouth Plantation 1608-1650 (Boston, Massachusetts: Massachusetts Historical Society, 1856; Boston, Massachusetts: Wright and Potter Printing Company, 1898, 1901, from the Original Manuscript, Library of Congress Rare Book Collection, Washington, D.C.; rendered in Modern English, Harold Paget, 1909

[13] Bradford, William. November 11, 1620, in the Mayflower Compact. William Bradford (Governor of Plymouth Colony), The History of Plymouth Plantation 1608-1650 (Boston, Massachusetts: Massachusetts Historical Society, 1856; Boston, Massachusetts: Wright and Potter Printing Company, 1898, 1901, from the Original Manuscript, Library of Congress Rare Book Collection, Washington, D.C.; rendered in Modern English, Harold Paget, 1909; NY: Russell and Russell, 1968; NY: Random House, Inc., Modern Library College edition, 1981; San Antonio, TX: American Heritage Classics, Mantle Ministries, 228 Still Ridge, Bulverde, Texas, 1988), pp. 75-76. Marshall Foster and Mary-Elaine Swanson, The American Covenant - The Untold Story (Roseburg, OR: Foundation for Christian Self-Government, 1981; Thousand Oaks, CA: The Mayflower Institute, 1983, 1992), p. vii. D.P. Diffine, Ph.D., One Nation Under God - How Close a Separation? (Searcy, Arkansas: Harding University, Belden Center for Private Enterprise Education, 6th edition, 1992), p. 3.

[14] Bradford, William. November 12, 1620, in recounting the Pilgrims' first full day in Cape Cod, Massachusetts, in his work entitled, The History of Plymouth Plantation 1608-1650 (Boston, Massachusetts: Massachusetts Historical Society, 1856; Boston, Massachusetts: Wright and Potter Printing Company, 1898, 1901, from the Original Manuscript, Library of Congress Rare Book

Collection, Washington, D.C.; rendered in Modern English, Harold Paget, 1909; NY: Russell and Russell, 1968; NY: Random House, Inc., Modern Library College edition, 1981; San Antonio, TX: American Heritage Classics, Mantle Ministries, 228 Still Ridge, Bulverde, Texas, 1988), ch. 9, p. 64. John Bartlett, Bartlett's Familiar Quotations (Boston: Little, Brown and Company, 1855, 1980), p. 265.

[15] Bradford, William. November 11, 1620, in his record of the Pilgrims' landing at Cape Cod, Massachusetts. William Bradford (Governor of Plymouth Colony), The History of Plymouth Plantation 1608-1650 (Boston, Massachusetts: Massachusetts Historical Society, 1856; Boston, Massachusetts: Wright and Potter Printing Company, 1898, 1901, from the Original Manuscript, Library of Congress Rare Book Collection, Washington, D.C.; rendered in Modern English, Harold Paget, 1909; NY: Russell and Russell, 1968; NY: Random House, Inc., Modern Library College edition, 1981; San Antonio, TX: American Heritage Classics, Mantle Ministries, 228 Still Ridge, Bulverde, Texas, 1988), p. 66

[16] Sacvan Bercovitch, ed., Typology and Early American Literature (Cambridge: University of Massachusetts Press, 1972), p. 104. Peter Marshall and David Manuel, The Glory of America (Bloomington, MN: Garborg's Heart 'N Home, Inc., 1991), 11.28. (note: reference to these first settlers as "pilgrims" is owed to this passage.)

[17] Bradford, William. 1650, in his work entitled, The History of Plymouth Plantation 1608-1650 (Boston, Massachusetts: Massachusetts Historical Society, 1856; Boston, Massachusetts: Wright and Potter Printing Company, 1898, 1901, from the Original Manuscript, Library of Congress Rare Book Collection, Washington, D.C.; rendered in Modern English, Harold Paget, 1909; NY: Russell and Russell, 1968; NY: Random House, Inc., Modern Library College edition, 1981; San Antonio, TX: American Heritage Classics, Mantle Ministries, 228 Still Ridge, Bulverde, Texas, 1988), p. 236. John Bartlett, Bartlett's Familiar Quotations (Boston: Little, Brown and Company, 1855, 1980), p. 265. Fleming, One Small Candle: The Pilgrim's First Year in America, p. 218.

[18] New Jersey, Seal of the Province of. 1697. Stephen K. McDowell and Mark A. Beliles, America's Providential History (Charlottesville, VA: Providence Press, 1989, 1994), p. 90.

[19] Bennett, Eilliam J., ed., The Spirit of America (Touchstone, Simon & Schuster Inc. 1997) pp. 42-43

The Pursuit of Happiness:
A Political Community

The American experiment was different in part due to one line that indicated one's right to "life, liberty, and the pursuit of happiness."

Today we do not understand that the pursuit of happiness was not intended for merely individual felicity, but indicated a sense of community that was indeed political. The word "politics" comes from the Greek word "polis" which indicated a self ruled city.

The sense of community and respect to others is a foundational concept of the American idea of opportunity for all to live safely in the society that was protected for the happiness of all. To fully understand this, we must go back again to the original settlers and examine their view of a polite city or community.

John Winthrop was the founder of the Massachusetts Bay Colony (1630), being elected 12 times consecutively as its governor. In England he was a member of the gentry, having been raised on a 500-acre estate his father had bought from Henry VIII. He had become a successful lawyer and strong Puritan leader. Oliver Cromwell pleaded with him to join the revolution against King Charles I, but he declined. He decided to flee for religious freedom, leading the English "Great Migration" to Salem in 1630. His journal, The History of New England, is a significant historical document. His son and grandson, both named John Winthrop, were also governors of Connecticut.

On May 15, 1629, in a letter to his wife, John Winthrop wrote:

Be of good comfort; the hardest that can come shall be a means to mortify this body of corruption, which is a thousand times more dangerous to us than any outward tribulation, and to bring us into nearer communion with our Lord Jesus Christ, and more assurance of His kingdom.[1]

The sense of eternal significance found in the colonists was certainly a basis of community. The community of believers together represented, in their eyes, an opportunity for happiness, or at least the pursuit thereof, without the intrusion of an oppressive government.

In June of 1630, ten years after the Pilgrims founded the Plymouth Colony; Governor John Winthrop founded the Holy Commonwealth of Massachusetts with 700 people sailing in eleven ships. This began the Great Migration, which saw more than twenty thousand Puritans embark for New England in the pursuing sixteen years.[2]

On June 11, 1630, aboard the Arbella, John Winthrop authored his work, A Model of Christian Charity, which became a guideline for future constitutional covenants of the Colonies:

It is of the nature and essence of every society to be knit together by some covenant, either expressed or implied...

This love among Christians is a real thing, not imaginary...as absolutely necessary to the being of the Body of Christ, as the sinews and other ligaments of a natural body are to the being of that body...

For the persons, we are a Company, professing ourselves fellow members of Christ, we ought to account ourselves knit together by this bond of love...For the work we have in hand, it is by a mutual consent through a special overruling Providence, and a more than an ordinary approbation of the Churches of Christ to seek out a place of Cohabitation and Consortship under a due form of Government both civil and ecclesiastical.

Therefore we must not content ourselves with usual ordinary means. Whatsoever we did or ought to have done when we lived in England, the same we must do, and more also where we go...Neither must we think that the Lord will bear such failings at our hands as He doth from those among whom we have lived...

Thus stands the cause between God and us: we are entered into covenant with Him for this work. We have taken out a Commission; the Lord hath given us leave to draw our own articles...

If the Lord shall please to hear us, and bring us in peace to the place we desire, then hath He ratified this Covenant and sealed our Commission, will expect a strict performance of the Articles...the Lord will surely break out in wrath against us. Now the only way to avoid this shipwreck and to provide for our posterity, is to follow the counsel of Micah, to do justly, to love mercy, to walk humbly with our God. For this end, we must be knit together in this work as one man. We must hold a familiar commerce together in each other in all meekness, gentleness, patience, and liberality.

We must delight in each other, make one another's condition our own, rejoice together, mourn together, labor and suffer together, always having before our eyes our Commission and Community in this work, as members of the same body. So shall we keep the unity of the Spirit in the bond of peace...

We shall find that the God of Israel is among us, when ten of us shall be able to resist a thousand of our enemies, when He shall make us a praise and glory, that men of succeeding plantations shall say, "The Lord make it like that of New England."

For we must Consider that we shall be as a City upon a Hill, the eyes of all people are upon us; so that if we shall deal falsely with our God in this work we have undertaken and so cause him to withdraw his present help from us, we shall be made a story and a by-word through the world, we shall open the mouths of enemies to speak evil of the ways of God and all professors for God's sake; we shall shame the faces of many of God's worthy servants, and cause their prayers to be turned into curses upon us till we be consumed out of the good land whether we are going. [3]

In his private journal, Governor John Winthrop wrote:

I will ever walk humbly before my God, and meekly, mildly, and gently towards all men...to give myself - my life, my wits, my health, my wealth –
to the service of my God and Saviour.[4]

Clearly for Governor John Winthrop his covenantal walk with God established his sense of community. Happiness was derived in community by expressing service to God through the attitudes of meekness, mildness and gentleness toward all men. Winthrop knew that such an ideal was inherently flawed because of the imperfect nature of men. The redemption of nature of God, however, allowed men to continue to turn their hearts toward God in the pursuit of happiness with other men.

"Teach me, O Lord, to put my trust in Thee, then shall I be like Mount Zion that cannot be moved...Before the week was gone...I waxed exceeding discontent and impatient...then I acknowledged my unfaithfulness and pride of heart, and turned again to my God, and humbled my soul before Him, and He returned and accepted me, and so I renewed my Covenant of walking with my God."[5]

The covenant between you and us is the oath you have taken of us, which is to this purpose, that we shall govern you and judge your causes by the rules of God's laws.[6]

On May 19, 1643, John Winthrop organized the New England Confederation among the Colonists of New Plymouth, New Haven, Massachusetts and Connecticut. They covenanted together under the Constitution of the New England Confederation:

Whereas we all came to these parts of America with the same end and aim, namely, to advance the kingdom of our Lord Jesus Christ, and to enjoy the liberties of the Gospel thereof with purities and peace, and for preserving and propagating the truth and liberties of the gospel.[7]

On December 15, 1617, in their letter to Sir Edwin Sandys in London, John Robinson and William Brewster explained that the Pilgrims were:

Knit together as a body in a most strict and sacred bond and covenant of the Lord, of the violation whereof we make great conscience, and by

virtue whereof we do hold ourselves straitly tied to all care of each other's good, and of the whole by every one and so mutually. [8]

Because of the nature of covenant faith, the pursuit of happiness is defined in terms of being "tied to all care of each other's good." The responsibility to the community as a whole is intrinsic to the pursuit of happiness. It is in this context that the framers of the Constitution said the juxtaposition of private rights and public happiness. In other words the pursuit of happiness had more to do with the happiness of the public as a whole while the right to life and liberty had to do with the private rights of individuals.

We see this concept advanced by James Madison, often referred to as the father of the Constitution, in his Federalist paper No. 14:

Is it not for glory of people of America, that while they have paid a decent regard to the opinions of former times and other nations, they have not suffered a blind confederation for antiquity, for custom, or for names, to overrule the suggestions of their own good sense, the knowledge of their own situation, and the lessons of their own experience? To this manly spirit, posterity will be indebted for the possession, and the world for the example of the numerous innovations displayed on the American theater, in favor of private rights and public happiness. Had no important step been taken by the leaders of the revolution for which a precedent could not be discovered, no government established of which an exact model did not present itself, but the United States might, at this moment, have been numbered among the melancholy victims of misguided councils, must at best have been laboring under the weight of some of those forms which have crushed the liberties of the rest of mankind. Happily for America, happily we trust for the whole human race, they pursued a new and more noble course, they accomplished a revolution which has no parallel in the annals of human society: they reared the fabrics of governments which have no model on the face of the globe. They formed the design of a great Confederacy, which is incumbent on their successors to improve and perpetuate.

The pursuit of happiness had been historically tied to freedom of worship. It was indeed the expression of happiness that the Pilgrims had found a place where people can be free to worship as they chose; this was so important to the community sense of the pursuit of happiness that it was not separated from the individual rights of life and liberty.

Roger Williams was a British-born clergyman who founded the Providence Plantation in Rhode Island. A graduate from Pembroke, 1624, he was ordained in the Church of England, 1628. An enthusiastic Puritan minister, his sermons in favor of religious liberty caused him to be persecuted. In 1630, he fled to the Massachusetts Bay Colony where he pastored in Plymouth, 1632-33, and in Salem, 1634. There his criticism of the state church led to a sentence of being sent back to England, 1635. He escaped and lived among the Indians, befriending them and learning their language.[9]

In 1636, he founded the town of Providence on land, which the Narragansett Indians gave him. **This was the first place where the freedom to worship God was separated from the control of the state.** In 1639, he organized the first Baptist Church in the new world, **with one of the principal foundations being that the state could not interfere with or restrict the free and open worship of God according to the Bible.** He sailed to England to obtain a patent for Rhode Island, 1643, and served as the colony's first President, 1654-57. In one of his messages, Roger Williams wrote:

When they have opened a gap in the hedge or wall of separation between the garden of the church and the wilderness of the world, God hath ever broken down the wall itself, removed the candlestick, and made His garden a wilderness, as at this day. And that therefore if He will enter please to restore His garden and paradise again, it must of necessity be walled in peculiarly unto Himself from the world.[10]

On January 9, 1872, Senator Henry Bowen Anthony delivered a eulogy of Roger Williams in Congress:

He knew, for God, whose prophet he was, revealed it to him, that the great principles for which he contended, and for which he suffered, founded in the eternal fitness of things, would endure forever.
He did not inquire if his name would survive a generation. In his vision of the future he saw mankind emancipated from...the blindness of bigotry,
from the cruelties of intolerance. He saw the nations walking forth into the liberty wherewith Christ had made them free.[11]

In his work, The Christian Commonwealth: or, The Civil Policy of the Rising Kingdom of Jesus Christ, 1659, which was a draft of a plan of government for the Natick Indian community, John Eliot stated:

That which the Lord now calleth England to attend is not to search humane Polities and Platformes of Government, contrived by the wisdom of man; but as the Lord hath carried on their works for them, so they ought to go unto the Lord and enquire at the Word of his mouth, what Platforme of Government he hath therein commanded; and humble themselves to embrace that as the best, how mean so ever it may seem to Humane Wisdom.

There is undoubtedly a form of Civil Government instituted by God himself in the Holy Scriptures; whereby any Nation may enjoy all the ends and effects of Government in the best manner, were they but persuaded to make trial of it. We should derogate from the sufficiency and perfection of the Scriptures, if we should deny it.
The Scripture is able thoroughly to furnish the man of God (whether Magistrate in the Commonwealth, or elder in the Church, or any other) unto every good work... Written Word of God is the perfect System or Frame of Laws, to guide all the Moral actions of man, either towards God or man.[12]

Again we find the consistent theme that the only way America's system of government will work is with a faith-based morality that constrains individuals from becoming too selfish because they have a code of behavior that is predictable in its responses towards God and man.

The second charter of Virginia reaffirms the understanding of the pursuit of happiness in a Christian context:

And forasmuch, as it shall be necessary for all such our loving Subjects, as shall inhabit within the said Precincts of Virginia, aforesaid, to determine to live together, in the Fear and true Worship of Almighty God, Christian Peace, and civil quietness, with each other, whereby every one may, with more Safety, Pleasure, and Profit, enjoy that, whereunto they shall attain with great Pain and Peril.[13]

John Locke was an English philosopher, diplomat and educator, whose writings had a profound influence on America's Founding Fathers. He received his master's degree from the Christ Church College of Oxford University, 1658, and lectured there on Greek, philosophy and rhetoric. He served as a diplomat to

Madrid, 1665, moved to France, 1675, then Holland, 1683, and returned to England, 1688. His works include: A Letter Concerning Toleration, 1689; Two Treatises of Government, 1690; An Essay Concerning Human Understanding, 1693; Some Thoughts Concerning Education, 1693; and The Reasonableness of Christianity, 1695. Of nearly 15,000 items of the Founding Fathers which were reviewed; including books, newspaper articles, pamphlets, monographs, etc., John Locke was the third most frequently quoted author. In his Two Treatises of Government, 1690, he cited 80 references to the Bible in the first treatise and 22 references to the Bible in the second.[14]

John Locke elaborated on fundamental concepts, such as: parental authority, separation of powers, private property, the right to resist unlawful authority, unalienable rights, and government by consent, whereby governments "derive their just powers from the consent of the governed."

Locke classified the basic natural rights of man as the right to "life, liberty and property." This not only influenced Thomas Jefferson, who penned the Declaration of Independence, but also elements in the Fifth and Fourteenth Amendments.

In his treatise Of Civil Government, 1689, John Locke stated:

Great and Chief End, therefore, of Men uniting into Commonwealths, and putting themselves under Government, is the preservation of their property…
For Men being all the Workmanship of one Omnipotent, and infinitely wise Maker: all the Servants of one Sovereign Master, sent into the World
by his Order, and about his Business, they are his Property, whose Workmanship they are, made to last during his, not one another's Pleasure…

Those Grants God made of the World to Adam, and to Noah, and his Sons...has given the Earth to the Children of Men, given it to Mankind in common... God, who hath given the World to Men in common, hath also given them reason to make use of it to the best Advantage of Life and Convenience.[15]

On August 23, 1689, in his work, Of Civil Government, John Locke wrote on natural law and natural rights:

The obligations of the Law of Nature cease not in society, but only in many cases are drawn closer, and have, by human laws, known penalties annexed to them to enforce their observation.
Thus the Law of Nature stands as an eternal rule to all men, legislators as well as others. The rules that they make for other men's actions must...
be conformable **to the Law of Nature; i.e. to the Will of God**, of which that is a declaration, and the fundamental Law of Nature being the
preservation of mankind, no human sanction can be good or valid against it.[16]

There are those today, in the blatant attempted secularization, which cite Locke as a foundational thinker for the founding fathers from the atheistic perspective of a naturalist. This myth must be debunked by the preceding reference, which clearly explains that when Locke (and his followers) used the term Law of Nature, they were referring to the Will of God and the right to life that is inherent in that will. Locke also subscribed to the golden rule as a key component to self-rule as it relates to the pursuit of happiness:

Our Saviour's great rule, that we should love our neighbors as ourselves, is such a fundamental truth for the regulating of human society, that, by

that alone, one might without difficulty determine all the cases and doubts in social morality.[17]

As the colonies realized that safety and welfare of the people were improved by cooperation between the communities, the pursuit of happiness for the community over the whole was advanced, as Christian principles of friendship and hospitality were the basis of cooperation.

The Constitution of the New England Confederation, (May 19, 1643), was the first document in America where colonies united themselves. The colonists of New Plymouth, New Haven, Massachusetts and Connecticut, covenanted together, stated:

The Articles of Confederation between the plantations under the government of Massachusetts, the plantations under the government of New Plymouth, the plantations under the government of Connecticut, and the government of New Haven with the plantations in combination therewith:
Whereas we all came to these parts of America with the same end and aim, namely, to advance the Kingdom of our Lord Jesus Christ, and to
enjoy the liberties of the Gospel thereof with purities and peace, and for preserving and propagating the truth and liberties of the gospel...
And whereas in our setting (by a wise providence of God) we are further dispersed upon the sea coasts and rivers than was at first intended...
The said United Colonies for themselves and their posterities to jointly and severely hereby **enter into a firm and perpetual league of friendship and amity for offence and defense, mutual advice and succor upon all just occasions both for preserving and propagating the Gospel and for their own mutual safety and welfare.**[18]

The supposition that morality and religion were vital supports to our system of government continued to be evident more than a century later when both the Declaration of Independence and the Constitution were formulated.

On January 1, 1769, Benjamin Franklin penned a letter to Lord James:

The moral character and happiness of mankind, are so interwoven with the operation of government, and the progress of the arts and sciences is so dependent on the nature of our political institutions, that it is essential to the advancement of civilized society to give ample discussion to these topics.[19]

William Bennett notes: "It is famously reported that upon the conclusion of the Constitutional Convention of 1787 a Mrs. Powell of Philadelphia asked of Benjamin Franklin "Well Doctor, what have we got a republic or a monarchy?" " A republic" replied the doctor, " if you can keep it." Unfortunately Franklin's challenge is hardly pondered today. And to the extent that it is, we answer that our political system is a machine that will go of itself, powered by such mechanisms as a separation of powers, federalism, institutional checks and balances, clashing political factions, free elections, pluralism, interest groups, and so on and so forth.

To some extent it does work this way, which was part of the founders plan. They believed that institutional arrangements would be central to the success of a modern Republic, and Americans are rightfully proud to possess the world's longest lasting and most imitated written political document -- -- the Constitution. Yet even with such extraordinary political instruments and institutions, the founders were aware that the American Republic would not, over the long haul, be so easily maintained.

From their study of history, the founders had learned of the travails of republic's before this one -- -- how the republics of old had, in time, been destroyed by convulsions and upheavals, by advice and decadence. And from their study of human nature, they became acutely aware of man's self interest and his selfishness, designing America's political institutions to take these into account. They concluded that while such institutional supports were absolutely necessary and could do much to rechannel and curb individual selfishness and discourage political convulsions, something more would be needed if the Republic was to survive. As John Adams put it, "Human passions unbridled by morality and religion would break the strongest cords of our Constitution as a whale goes through a net." [20]

It was Adams while serving his second term as vice president, some 20 years after the signing of the Declaration of Independence, who captured this concept succinctly in his diary:

One great advantages of the Christian religion is that it brings the great principle of the Law of nature and nations -- -- love your neighbor as yourself, and do to others as you would that others should do to you, -- -- to the knowledge, belief, and veneration of the whole people. Children, servants, women, and men, are all professors in the science of public and private morality. No other institution for education, no kind of political discipline, could diffuse this kind of necessary information, so universally among all ranks and descriptions of citizens. The duties and rights of the men and the citizens are thus taught from early infancy to every creature. The sanctions of the future life are thus added to the observance of civil and political, as well as domestic and private duties. Prudence, justice, temperance, and fortitude, are thus taught to be the means and conditions of future as well as present happiness.

Adams held to the belief that the morality and religious foundation that would undergird our system of government is not merely inherited but must be taught; and so teach we must.

---

[1] Winthrop, John. May 15, 1629, in a letter to his wife. Appleton's Cyclopedia of American Biography, Vol. VI. Stephen Abbott Northrop, D.D., A Cloud of Witnesses (Portland, OR: American Heritage Ministries, 1987; Mantle Ministries, 228 Still Ridge, Bulverde, Texas), p. 516.

[2] Winthrop, John. Peter Marshall and David Manuel, The Light and the Glory (Old Tappan, NJ: Fleming H. Revell Company, 1977), p. 148.

[3] Winthrop, John. 1630, "A Model of Christian Charity." Stewart Mitchell, editor, The Winthrop Papers, 1623-1630 (Boston: Massachusetts Historical Society, 1931), Vol. II, pp. 292-295. John Bartlett, Bartlett's Familiar Quotations (Boston: Little, Brown and Company, 1855, 1980), p. 264. Perry Miller and Thomas H. Johnson, The Puritans: A Sourcebook of Their Writings, Vol. I (New York: Harper & Row, 1938, 1963), pp. 195-199. John Eidsmoe, Christianity and the Constitution - The Faith of Our Founding Fathers (Grand Rapids, MI: Baker Book House, A Mott Media Book, 1987, 6th printing 1993), pp. 29-30. Peter Marshall and David Manuel, The Light and the Glory (Old Tappan, NJ: Fleming H. Revell Company, 1977), pp. 161-162. Francis W. Coker, ed., Democracy, Liberty, and Property: Readings in the American Political Tradition (NY: The Macmillan Co., 1942), pp. 18-20. Marshall Foster and Mary-Elaine Swanson, The American Covenant - The Untold Story (Roseburg, OR: Foundation for Christian Self-Government, 1981; Thousand Oaks, CA: The Mayflower Institute, 1983, 1992), p. 80. Mark A. Noll, et al., eds., Eerdmans' Handbook to Christianity in America (Grand Rapids, MI: William B. Eerdmans Publishing Company, 1983), p. 38. Gary DeMar, The Biblical Worldview (Atlanta, GA: An American Vision Publication - American Vision, Inc., 1993), Vol. 9, No. 2, p. 13. Gary DeMar, America's Christian History: The Untold Story (Atlanta, GA: American Vision Publishers, Inc., 1993), p. 5. Stephen McDowell and Mark Beliles, "The Providential Perspective" (Charlottesville, VA: The Providence Foundation, P.O. Box 6759, Charlottesville, Va. 22906, January 1994), Vol. 9, No. 1, p. 2. The Annals of America, 20 vols. (Chicago, IL: Encyclopedia Britannica, 1968), Vol. I, pp. 109-115. Charles H. Lippy, et als., Christianity Comes to the Americas, 1492-1776 (NY: Paragon House, 1989), p. 265.

[4] Winthrop, John. 1598-1628, writing in his Journal. The Winthrop Papers (Boston: Massachusetts Historical Society, 1929), Vol. I, pp. 196, 201.

[5] Winthrop, John. Winthrop Papers, Vol. II, pp. 292-295. Peter Marshall and David Manuel, The Glory of America (Bloomington, MN: Garborg's Heart'N Home, Inc., 1991), 3.26.

[6] Winthrop, John. 1645. Charles Hurd, ed., A Treasury of Great American Speeches (NY: Hawthorne Books, 1959), p. 18.

[7] Winthrop, John. May 19, 1643, in the Constitution of the New England Confederation. Benjamin Franklin Morris, The Christian Life and Character of the Civil Institutions of the United States (Philadelphia, PA: L. Johnson & Co., 1863; George W. Childs, 1864), p. 56. William McDonald,

ed., Documentary Source Book of American History 1606-1889 (NY: The Macmillan Company, 1909), p. 46. Henry Steele Commager, ed., Documents of American History, 2 vols. (NY: F.S. Crofts and Company, 1934; Appleton-Century-Crofts, Inc., 1948, 6th edition, 1958; Englewood Cliffs, NJ: Prentice Hall, Inc., 9th edition, 1973), p. 26. Gary DeMar, God and Government (Atlanta, GA: American Vision Press, 1984), p. 112. "Our Christian Heritage," Letter from Plymouth Rock (Marlborough, NH: The Plymouth Rock Foundation), p. 2.

[8] Bradford, William. December 15, 1617, in a letter from John Robinson and William Brewster in Leyden, Holland, to Sir Edwin Sandys in London, England. William Bradford (Governor of Plymouth Colony), The History of Plymouth Plantation 1608-1650 (Boston, Massachusetts: Massachusetts Historical Society, 1856; Boston, Massachusetts: Wright and Potter Printing Company, 1898, from the original manuscript; rendered in Modern English, Harold Paget, 1909; NY: Russell and Russell, 1968; San Antonio, TX: American Heritage Classics, Mantle Ministries, 228 Still Ridge, Bulverde, Texas, 1988), p.28.

[9] Williams, Roger, The World Book Encyclopedia, 18 vols. (Chicago, IL: Field Enterprises, Inc., 1957; W.F. Quarrie and Company, 8 vols., 1917; World Book, Inc., 22 vols., 1989), Vol. 14, p. 6931.

[10] Williams, Roger, Lynn R. Buzzard and Samuel Ericsson, The Battle for Religious Liberty (Elgin, IL: David C. Cook, 1982), p. 51. John Eidsmoe, Christianity and the Constitution - The Faith of Our Founding Fathers (Grand Rapids, MI: Baker Book House, A Mott Media Book, 1987, 6th printing 1993), pp. 215, 243.

[11] Wliams, Roger. January 9, 1872, Senator Henry Bowen Anthony delivers the Eulogy of Roger Williams in Congress. Stephen Abbott Northrop, D.D., A Cloud of Witnesses (Portland, Oregon: American Heritage Ministries, 1987; Mantle Ministries, 228 Still Ridge, Bulverde, Texas), p. 16.

[12] Eliot, John. 1659 John Eliot, The Christian Commonwealth: or, The Civil Policy of the Rising Kingdom of Jesus Christ, 1659. John Eliot, Massachusetts Historical Collections, 3rd ser,. Vol. 9, pp. 133-134, 163. Benjamin Fletcher Wright, Jr., American Interpretations of Natural Law (NY: Russell & Russell, 1962), pp. 19-21. John Eidsmoe, Christianity and the Constitution - The Faith of Our Founding Fathers (Grand Rapids, MI: Baker Book House, A Mott Media Book, 1987; 6th printing, 1993), pp. 33-34. Gary DeMar, America's Christian History: The Untold Story (Atlanta, GA: American Vision Publishers, Inc., 1993), pp. 125-126.

[13] Eliot, John. 1659 John Eliot, The Christian Commonwealth: or, The Civil Policy of the Rising Kingdom of Jesus Christ, 1659. John Eliot, Massachusetts Historical Collections, 3rd ser,. Vol. 9, pp. 133-134, 163. Benjamin Fletcher Wright, Jr., American Interpretations of Natural Law (NY: Russell & Russell, 1962), pp. 19-21. John Eidsmoe, Christianity and the Constitution - The Faith of Our Founding Fathers (Grand Rapids, MI: Baker Book House, A Mott Media Book, 1987; 6th printing, 1993), pp. 33-34. Gary DeMar, America's Christian History: The Untold Story (Atlanta, GA: American Vision Publishers, Inc., 1993), pp. 125-126.

[14] Locke, John. Donald S. Lutz and Charles S. Hyneman, "The Relative Influence of European Writers on Late Eighteenth-Century American Political Thought," American Political Review 189 (1984): 189-197. (Courtesy of Dr. Wayne House of Dallas Theological Seminary.) John Eidsmoe,

Christianity and the Constitution - The Faith of Our Founding Fathers (Grand Rapids, MI: Baker Book House, A Mott Media Book, 1987, 6th printing 1993), pp. 51-53. Stephen K. McDowell and Mark A. Beliles, America's Providential History (Charlottesville, VA: Providence Press, 1988), p. 156. [1760-1805], Origins of American Constitutionalism, (1987).

[15] Locke, John. 1689, in his work Of Civil Government. John Locke, Two Treatises on Civil Government (London: George Routledge and Sons, 1903) Book 2, p. 262. John Locke, The Second Treatise Of Civil Government 1690 (Reprinted Buffalo, NY: Prometheus Books, 1986) p. 77. Frank Donovan, Mr. Jefferson's Declaration (New York: Dodd Mead & Co., 1968), p. 137. Pat Robertson, America's Dates with Destiny (Nashville: Thomas Nelson Publishers, 1986), p. 66. Verna M. Hall, Christian History of the Constitution of the United States of America (San Francisco: Foundation for American Christian Education, 1975), pp. 58, 63-64, 91. Marshall Foster and Mary-Elaine Swanson, The American Covenant - The Untold Story (Roseburg, OR: Foundation for Christian Self-Government, 1981; Thousand Oaks, CA: The Mayflower Institute, 1983, 1992), pp. 111-112.

[16] Locke, John. August 23, 1689, in his work Of Civil Government. John Locke, The Second Treatise on Civil Government, 1690 (reprinted Buffalo, NY: Prometheus Books, 1986), p. 75. John Locke, Two Treatises on Civil Government (London: George Routledge and Sons, 1903), Book 2, p. 262. Verna M.Hall, The Christian History of the Constitution of the United States of America - Christian Self-Government with Union (San Francisco: Foundation for American Christian Education, 1976), p. 58. Marshall Foster and Mary-Elaine Swanson, The American Covenant - The Untold Story (Roseburg, OR: Foundation for Christian Self-Government, 1981; Thousand Oaks, CA: The Mayflower Institute, 1983, 1992), p. 108.

[17] Locke, John. 1695, John Locke, A Vindication of the Reasonableness of Christianity, a paraphrase of the books of Romans, First and Second Corinthians, Galatians and Ephesians. John Churchill, The Works of John Locke, Esq., 3 Vol. (1714). Verna M. Hall, The Christian History of the Constitution of the United States of America - Christian Self-Government with Union (San Francisco: Foundation for American Christian Education, 1976), Vol. I, op cit, 56. Russ Walton, One Nation Under God (NH: Plymouth Rock Foundation, 1993), p. 22.

[18] New England Confederation, Constitution of the. May 19, 1643. Ebenezer Hazard, Historical Collection: Consisting of State Papers and other Authentic Documents: Intended as Materials for an History of the United States of America (Philadelphia: T. Dobson, 1792), Vol. II, p. 1. Benjamin Franklin Morris, The Christian Life and Character of the Civil Institutions of the United States (Philadelphia: George W. Childs, 1864), p. 56. Henry Steele Commager, ed., Documents of American History, 2 vols. (NY: F.S. Crofts and Company, 1934; Appleton-Century-Crofts, Inc., 1948, 6th edition, 1958; Englewood Cliffs, NJ: Prentice Hall, Inc., 9th edition, 1973), Vol. I, pp. 26-27. William McDonald, ed., Documentary Source Book of American History, 1606-1889 (NY: The Macmillan Company, 1909), p. 46. William Bradford (Governor of Plymouth Colony), The History of Plymouth Plantation 1608-1650 (Boston, Massachusetts: Massachusetts Historical Society, 1856; Boston, Massachusetts: Wright and Potter Printing Company, 1898, 1901, from the Original Manuscript, Library of Congress Rare Book Collection, Washington, D.C.; rendered in Modern English, Harold Paget, 1909; NY: Russell and Russell, 1968; NY: Random House, Inc., Modern Library College edition, 1981; San Antonio, TX: American Heritage Classics, Mantle Ministries, 228 Still Ridge, Bulverde, Texas, 1988), pp. 321-324. The Annals of America, 20 vols. (Chicago, IL: Encyclopedia Britannica, 1968), Vol. 1, pp. 72-73. Gary DeMar, God and Government (Atlanta,

GA: American Vision Press, 1984), p. 112. Lucille Johnston, Celebrations of a Nation (Arlington, VA: The Year of Thanksgiving Foundation, 1987), (part 1), p. 46. "Our Christian Heritage," Letter from Plymouth Rock (Marlborough, NH: The Plymouth Rock Foundation), p. 2. D.P. Diffine, Ph.D., One Nation Under God - How Close a Separation? (Searcy, Arkansas: Harding University, Belden Center for Private Enterprise Education, 6th edition, 1992), p. 4. Gary DeMar, America's Christian History: The Untold Story (Atlanta, GA: American Vision Publishers, Inc., 1993), pp. 37-38.

[19] Franklin, Benjamin. January 1, 1769, in a letter to Lord James. Paul W. Connor, Poor Richard's Politiks - Benjamin Franklin and His American Order (NY: Oxford University Press, 1965), p. 107. John Eidsmoe, Christianity and the Constitution - The Faith of Our Founding Fathers (Grand Rapids, MI: Baker Book House, A Mott Media Book, 1987; 6th printing, 1993), p. 211.

[20] Bennett, William J., ed., The Spirit of America (Touchstone, Simon & Schuster Inc. 1997), pp. 15-16.

True Justice:
A Common Higher Authority

The premise that God ordained successful self-rule in order to free people from tyranny and oppression undergirded much of the initial intents of the colonies.

The Great Law of Pennsylvania (December 7, 1682), the first legislative act of Pennsylvania, stated:

Whereas the glory of Almighty God and the good of mankind is the reason and the end of government, and, therefore government itself is a venerable Ordinance of God....[let there be established] laws as shall best preserve true Christian and Civil liberty, in opposition to all unchristian, licentious, and unjust practices, whereby God may have his due, and Caesar his due, and the people their due, from tyranny and oppression. [1]

The American system of law and justice was likewise rooted in faith. One of the first protections of law was against religious persecution and/or state sponsored religion or indoctrination:

That no person, now or at any time hereafter, Living in this Province, who shall confess and acknowledge one Almighty God to be the Creator, Upholder and Ruler of the World, And who professes, him or herself Obliged in Conscience to live peaceably and quietly under the civil government, shall in any case be molested or prejudiced for his, or her Conscientious persuasion or practice.

Nor shall he or she at any time be compelled to frequent or maintain any religious worship, place of Ministry whatever, Contrary to his, or her

mind, but shall freely and fully enjoy his, or her, Christian Liberty in that respect, without any Interruption or reflection.

And if any person shall abuse or deride any other, for his, or her different persuasion and practice in matters of religion, such person shall be

looked upon as a Disturber of the peace, and be punished accordingly.[2]

Today the tables are turned. It has practically become in vogue or chic to not only question but actually renounce the rights of Christian's as it pertains to public displays of their faith. Public schools permit Muslim children to kneel to the east and pray in the name of Allah five times a day while Christian children are rebuked for the mere mention of the name of Jesus in a written classroom assignment.

The judicial branch has consistently assumed more and more power especially where it relates to matters of religion. The secularization of our system of law also does not bode well for its future success. Like civility and the pursuit of happiness, our inherent judicial differences such as "innocent until proven guilty", "the right to a trial by a jury of your peers", etc. have been "interpreted away". The broader challenge stems from a parallel move in the courts away from our premise of faith-based morality.

To avoid superfluous commentary, one need only look again to the historical roots of our system of jurisprudence. In this chapter, we will take a look at some of the words that framed the lives of individuals who had a profound impact on the establishment of our system of laws and jurisprudence.

Hugo Grotius was a Dutch jurist, theologian and statesman, who was **considered the founder of the science of International Law**. In 1607, being 24 years old, he was appointed Advocate General for the provinces of Holland and Zealand. In 1613, at the age of 30, he became the Chief Magistrate of Rotterdam. In 1619, Prince Maurice of Nassau sentenced him to life imprisonment for his support of the Armenian faith. Three years later, with his wife's help, he escaped to France hidden in a linen chest. Hugo Grotius (or Huig de Groot in the Dutch language), published De Jure Belli et Pacis (On the Law of War and Peace), in 1625, which was a study of the laws of mankind in reference to individuals, nations and states. From 1635 until his death he served as the Swedish ambassador to France. President James Madison described him as: The father of the modern code of nations.[3]

In his work, On the Law of War and Peace, Hugo Grotius stated:

Among all good men one principle at any rate is established beyond controversy, that if the authorities issue any order that is contrary to the law of nature or to the commandments of God, the order should not be carried out. For when the Apostles said that obedience should be rendered to God rather than men, they appealed to an infallible rule of action, which is written in the hearts of all men.[4].

As a core value for international law that inspired the founding fathers of the United States, obedience to a higher authority than man's authority is essential.

What motivation is there for someone to honor their oath to tell the truth, the whole truth and nothing but the truth, so help you God if you don't believe that God exists? Or how can someone who believes there is no absolute truth vow to tell the truth in court if their philosophy states that they don't know that anything is absolutely true?

If it were not permitted to punish certain Criminals with Death, nor to defend the Subject by Arms against Highwaymen and Pyrates, there would of Necessity follow a terrible Inundation of Crimes, and a Deluge of Evils, since even now that Tribunals are erected, it is very difficult to restrain the
Boldness of profligate Persons.

Wherefore if it had been the Design of CHRIST to have introduced a new Kind of Regulation, as was never heard of before, he would certainly have declared in most distinct and plain Words, that none should pronounce Sentence of Death against a Malefactor, or carry Arms in Defense of one's Country.[5]

Especially, however, Christian kings and states are bound to pursue this method of avoiding wars...Both for this and for other reasons it would be advantageous to hold certain conferences of Christian powers, where those who have no interest at stake may settle the disputes of others, and where,
in fact, steps may be taken to compel parties to accept peace on fair terms.[6]

Grotius stated what may seem to be the obvious but was not at the time, and, in fact, is not as widely held today as it perhaps should be:

He knows not how to rule a kingdome, that cannot manage a Province; nor can he wield a Province, that cannot order a City; nor he order a City, that

knows not how to regulate a Village; nor he a Village, that cannot guide a Family; nor can that man Govern well a Family that knows not how to Govern himselfe; neither can any Govern himselfe unless reason be Lord, Will and Appetite her Vassals: nor can Reason rule unlesse herselfe be ruled by God, and (wholy) be obedient to Him.[7]

In the closing remarks of The Rights of War and Peace, Grotius wrote:

May God, who alone hath the power, inscribe these teachings on the hearts of those who hold sway over the Christian world, may He grant to them a mind possessing knowledge of divine and human law, and having ever before it the reflection that it hath been chosen as a servant for the rule of
man, the living thing most dear to God.[8]

As he worked his way back to the basics of true justice, In his Commentary on the Law of Prize and Booty, Hugo Grotius stated:

Whatever God has shown to be his will that is Law.[9]

In his second work, The Truth of the Christian Religion, Hugo Grotius wrote:

There is no reason for Christians to doubt the credibility of these Books (of the Bible), because there are testimonies in our books out of almost every one of them, the same as they are found in the Hebrew.
Nor did Christ, when He reproved many things in the teachings of the Law, and in the Pharisees of His time, ever accuse them of falsifying the
Books of Moses and the Prophets, or of using supposititious or altered books.

And it can never be proved, or made credible, that after Christ's time the Scripture should be corrupted in anything of moment, if we consider how far and wide the Jewish nation, who everywhere kept these Books, was dispersed over the whole world.[10]

John Cotton was a powerful Puritan minister and scholar in Boston, Massachusetts. Born in England, he fled to the colonies in 1632 to avoid religious persecution. There he rose to become **perhaps the most influential leader in shaping the destiny of Puritan New England**, serving at the First Church of Boston, 1633-52. Known for his didactic writings, the principles stated in his sermons were frequently put into immediate practice by civil authorities.

In 1636, Rev. John Cotton gave the outline for a code of laws, which included the phrase:

The Law of Nature, delivered by God. [11]

He ended his work with the Scripture reference, Isaiah 33:22:

The Lord is our Judge.
The Lord is our Law-giver.
The Lord is our King, He will save us[12]

In reflection on the human tendency to be corrupted by power, Rev. John Cotton stated:

Let all the world learn to give mortall men no greater power than they are content they shall use, for use it they will: and unless they be better taught of God, they will use it ever and anon....

For whatever transcendent power is given, will certainly over-run those that give it, and those that receive it: there is a straine in a mans heart that

will sometime or other runne out to excesse, unlesse the Lord restraine it, but it is not good to venture it: It is necessary therefore, that all power that is on

earth be limited, Church-power or other...

It is counted a matter of danger to the State to limit Prerogatives; but it is a further danger, not to have them limited: They will be like a Tempest, if

they be not limited: A Prince himselfe cannot tell where he will confine himselfe, nor can the people tell....

It is therefore fit for every man to be studious of the bounds which the Lord hath set: and for the People, in whom fundamentally all power lyes, to

give as much power as God in his word gives to men:

And it is meet that Magistrates in the commonwealth, and so Officers in Churches should desire to know the utmost bounds of their own power,

and it is safe for both:

All intrenchment upon the bounds which God hath not given, they are not enlargements, but burdens and snares: They will certainly lead the spirit

of a man out of his way sooner or later.

It is wholesome and safe to be dealt withall as God deales with the vast Sea;

Hitherto shalt thou come, but there shalt thou stay thy proud waves:

and therefore if they be but banks of simple sand, they will be good enough to check the vast roaring Sea.[13]

    Cotton expressed the need for biblical boundaries to insure that jurisprudence would be just that—the wisdom of justice. He declared:

What He hath planted, He will maintain. Every plantation His right hand hath not planted shall be rooted up, but His own plantation shall prosper and flourish.

When He promiseth peace and safety, what enemies shall be able to make the promise of God of none effect? Neglect not wall and bulwarks and fortifications for your own defense, but ever let the name of the Lord be your strong tower, and the word of His promise, the rock of your refuge.

His word that made heaven and earth will not fail, till heaven and earth be no more....

If God make a covenant to be a God to thee and thine, then it is thy part to see to it that thy children and servants be God's people. [14]

Thomas Hooker was the founder of Hartford, Connecticut in 1636. A Cambridge University graduate, Thomas Hooker was persecuted in England after having gotten involved with the Christian movement known as the Puritans. Exiled from England for his religious beliefs, he fled first to Holland, then to Massachusetts (1633), where he became the minister at the Cambridge (formerly New-Town) settlement. Disputes with the Massachusetts leadership drove him and his congregation to Connecticut.

In 1638, he stated to the Connecticut General Assembly that he believed people had a God-given right to choose their magistrates. He was a principal organizer of the New England colonies into the defensive confederation, known as the United Colonies of New England, 1643. In 1648, he wrote A Survey of the Summe of Church Discipline.

An influential leader, Thomas Hooker's sermon before the General Court of Connecticut put forth such unprecedented democratic principles, that it inspired the writing of the Fundamental Constitutions of Connecticut in 1639. **This constitution inspired ideas of individual rights, such as: "due process of law," "trial by a jury of peers," "no taxation without representation" and prohibitions against "cruel and unusual punishment." It later became a model for all other constitutions in the colonies, including the United States Constitution.**[15]

In 1638, Rev. Thomas Hooker accentuated:
The choice of public magistrates belongs unto the people, by God's allowance...(T)he privilege of election, which belongs to the people, therefore must not be exercised according to their humours, but according to the blessed will and law of God.[16]

Today, the law of God is nearly never referred to in terms of public discussion surrounding the conditions of our courts and the judiciary as a whole. One of the most influential elements of American history dealt directly with the issue of the law of God as opposed to the presumed authority in the law of kings.

Samuel Rutherford was Rector of St. Andrew's Church in Scotland and one of the commissioners at Westminster Assembly in London from 1643-47. In 1644, he wrote the controversial book, ***Lex, Rex*** or, *The Law and the Prince*, which challenged the "divine right of kings."

Instead of the king being God's appointed regent whose word is law, Rutherford stated that all men, even the king, were under the law and not above it. He reasoned that even though rulers derived their authority from God by Romans 13:1-4, they received their authority through the people.

Samuel Rutherford cited the following biblical passages in support:

II Samuel 16:18, "Hushai said to Absalom, Nay, but whom the Lord and the people, and all the men of Israel choose, his will I be, and with him will I abide";

Judges 8:22, "The men of Israel said to Gideon, Rule thou over us";

Judges 9:6, "The men of Shechem made Abimelech king";

II Kings 14:21, "The people made Azariah king";

I Samuel 12:1, "Now Samuel said to all Israel: 'Indeed I have heeded your voice in all that you said to me, and have made a king over you.'";

II Chronicles 23:3, "Then all the assembly made a covenant with the king in the house of God."[17]

This book brought immediate opposition, being banned in Scotland and publicly burned in England. Rutherford was placed under house arrest and summoned to trial before the Parliament in Edinburgh. He died before the orders could be carried out. In his book, Lex, Rex, Samuel Rutherford introduced the phrase:

All men are created equal.[18]

This phrase flew in the face of the nobles. Whether aristocratic by birth or by appointment, the existing power structure was immediately threatened by the idea of equality in creation that should equal equality of opportunity. Elected officials' roles and relationships to their fellow man would need to be redefined.

In 1645, John Winthrop defined the duties of elected officials:

The great questions that have troubled the country are about the authority of the magistrates and the liberty of the people.

It is yourselves who have called us to this office, and, being called by you, we have our authority from God, in way of ordinance, such as hath the image of God eminently stamped upon it, the contempt and violation whereof hath been vindicated with examples of divine vengeance. [19]

One of the most influential thinkers of his day, John Locke took a keen interest in how men's matters would be governed. He was an English philosopher, diplomat and educator, whose writings had a profound influence on America's Founding Fathers. He received his master's degree from the Christ Church College of Oxford University, 1658, and lectured there on Greek, philosophy and rhetoric. He served as a diplomat to Madrid, 1665, moved to France, 1675, then Holland, 1683, and returned to England, 1688. His works include: A Letter Concerning Toleration, 1689; Two Treatises of Government, 1690; An Essay Concerning Human Understanding, 1693; Some Thoughts Concerning Education, 1693; and The Reasonableness of Christianity, 1695.

Of nearly 15,000 items of the Founding Fathers which were reviewed; including books, newspaper articles, pamphlets, monographs, etc., John Locke was the third most frequently quoted author.[20] In his Two Treatises of Government, 1690, he cited 80 references to the Bible in the first treatise and 22 references to the Bible in the second.

John Locke elaborated on fundamental concepts, such as: parental authority, separation of powers, private property, the right to resist unlawful authority, unalienable rights, and government by consent, whereby governments "derive their just powers from the consent of the governed." Concerning the idea of a "social compact," a constitution between the people and the government, John Locke traced its origins to:

That Paction which God made with Noah after the Deluge. [21]

John Locke classified the basic natural rights of man as the right to "life, liberty and property." This not only influenced Thomas Jefferson, who penned the Declaration of Independence, but also elements in the Fifth and Fourteenth Amendments.

In his treatise Of Civil Government, 1689, John Locke stated:

Great and Chief End, therefore, of Mens uniting into Commonwealths, and putting themselves under Government, is the preservation of their property....

For Men being all the Workmanship of one Omnipotent, and infinitely wise Maker: all the Servants of one Sovereign Master, sent into the World by his Order, and about his Business, they are his Property, whose Workmanship they are, made to last during his, not one another's Pleasure....

Those Grants God made of the World to Adam, and to Noah, and his Sons...has given the Earth to the Children of Men, given it to Mankind in common...

God, who hath given the World to Men in common, hath also given them reason to make use of it to the best Advantage of Life and Convenience.

On August 23, 1689, in his work, Of Civil Government, John Locke wrote on natural law and natural rights:

The obligations of the Law of Nature cease not in society, but only in many cases are drawn closer, and have, by human laws, known penalties annexed to them to enforce their observation. Thus the Law of Nature stands as an eternal rule to all men, legislators as well as others. The rules that they make for other men's actions Must...be conformable to the Law of Nature; i.e. to the Will of God, of which that is a declaration, and the fundamental Law of Nature being the preservation of mankind, no human sanction can be good or valid against it. [22]

Massachusetts General Court (1636), resolved to establish a code of laws that would be: **agreeable to the word of God**[23].

Connecticut General Court (1639), established under the Constitution of Connecticut, issued the order:

That God's word should be the only rule for ordering the affairs of government in this commonwealth.

The Fundamental Orders (Constitution) of Connecticut (January 14, 1639) was the first constitution written in America, establishing a pattern which all others followed, including the United States Constitution.[24] It was penned by Roger Ludlow, 1638, after hearing a sermon by Thomas Hooker, the Puritan minister who founded Hartford, Connecticut. So important was this work that Connecticut became known as "The Constitution State".[25] The committee responsible to frame the orders was charged to make the laws:

As near the law of God as they can be[26]

On January 14, 1639, the Connecticut towns of Hartford, Wethersfield and Windsor adopted the constitution, which stated in its Preamble:

Forasmuch as it has pleased the Almighty God by the wise disposition of His divine providence so to order and dispose of things that we the inhabitants and residents of Windsor, Hartford and Wethersfield and now cohabiting and dwelling in and upon the River Connecticut and the lands thereunto adjoining;
and well knowing when a people are gathered together the Word of God requires, that to meinteine the peace and union of such a people, there

should bee an orderly and decent government established according to God, to order and dispose of the affairs of all the people at all seasons as occasion shall require;

do therefore associate and conjoin ourselves to be as one public State or Commonwealth, and do, for ourselves and our successors and such as shall be adjoined to us at any time hereafter, enter into Combination and Confederation together, to meinteine and presearve the libberty and purity of the Gospell of our Lord Jesus which we now professe, as also the discipline of the churches,

Which, according to the truth of the said Gospell, is now practised amongst us; as allso, in our civill affaires to be guided and governed according to such lawes, rules, orders, and decrees....

I. It is ordered, sentenced and decreed, that there shall be yearly two General Assemblies...wherein shall be yearly chosen from time to time so Many Magistrates and other public Officers as shall be found requiste...which being chosen and sworne according to an Oath recorded for that purpose shall have power to administer justice according to the Laws here established, and for want thereof according to the rule of the Word of God....

The Oath of the Governor: "I, N.W., being now chosen to be Governor within this jurisdiction, for the year ensuing, and until a new be chosen, do swear by the great and dreadful name of the everliving God, to promote the public good and peace of the same, according to the best of my skill; as also will maintain all lawful priviledges of this Commonwealth; **as also that all wholesome laws that are or shall be made by lawful authority here established, be duly executed; and will further the execution of Justice according to the rule of God's Word; so help me God, in the name of the Lord Jesus Christ."** [27]

Massachusetts Bay Colony, Cambridge Platform of the (1648), recorded in the Plymouth Colony Records IX, 1663, listed the proposal of William Vassall and others:

1. CHAP: XVII: Of The Civil Magistrates power in Matters Ecclesiastical...It is lawfull, profitable, & necessary for Christians to gather themselves into Church estate, and therein to exercise all the ordinances of Christ according unto the word, because the Apostles & Christians in their time did frequently thus practise, when the Magistrates being all of them Jewish or pagan, & mostly persecuting enemies, would give no countenance or consent to such matters.

2. Church-government stands in no opposition to civil government of commonwealths, nor any intrencheth upon the authority of civil Magistrates in their jurisdictions; nor any wit weakeneth their hands in governing; but rather strengthneth them, & furthereth the people in yielding more hearty and conscionable obedience unto them, whatsoever some ill affected persons to the wayes of Christ have suggested to alienate the affections of Kings & Princes from the ordinences of Christ; **as if the kingdome of Christ in his church could not rise & stand, without the falling and weakening of their government**, which is also of Christ: whereas the contrary is most true, that they may both stand together & flourish the one being helpful to the other, in distinct and due administrations.

3. The power & authority of Magistrates is not for the restraining of churches, or any other good workes, but for helping in and furthering therof; & therfore the consent & contenance of Magistrates when it may be had, is not to be slighted, or lightly esteemed; but on the contrary; it is part of that honour due to Christian Magistrates to desire & crave their consent & approbation therin: which being

obtayned, the churches may then proceed in their way with much more encouragement, & comfort.

4. It is not in the power of Magistrates to compell their subjects to become churchmembers, & to partake at the Lord's table:..Those whom the church is to cast out if they were in, the Magistrates ought not to thrust into the church, nor to hold them therin.

5. **As it is unlawful for church-officers to meddle with the sword of the Magistrates, so is it unlawfull for the Magistrates to meddle with the work proper to church-officers...**

6. It is the duty of the Magistrate, to take care of matters of religion, & to improve his civil authority for the observing of the duties commanded in the first, as well as for observing the duties commanded in the second table...

7. Idolatry, Blasphemy, Heresy, venting corrupt & pernicious opinions, that destroy the foundation, open contempt of the word preached, prophanation of the Lord's day, disturbing the peaceable administration & exercise of the worship & holy things of God, & the like, are to be restrayned, & punished by civil authority.

8. If any church one or more shall grow schismaticall, rending it self from the communion of other churched, or shall walke incorrigibly or obstinately in any corrupt way of their own, contrary to the rule of the word; in such a case, the Magistrate is to put forth his coercive powr, as the matter shall require. The tribes on this side Jordan intended to make warr against the other tribes, for building the altar of witness, whom they suspected to have turned away therin from following of the Lord, Finis.[28]

This document showed the attitude of not only peaceful co-existence between church and courts, but of cooperation.

But when we speak of our founding fathers, the faith in Christ they had, and how it effected the establishment of this nation, specifically, the legislative and judicial areas, the name of a self-taught lawyer turned senator who then turned judge truly stands out.

Roger Sherman was an American Revolutionary patriot, jurist and politician. **He was distinguished as the only Founding Father to sign all four major founding documents: The Articles of Association, 1774; The Declaration of Independence, 1776; The Articles of Confederation, 1777; and The Constitution of the United States, 1787.**

Roger Sherman was a shoe cobbler, surveyor and merchant prior to his political career. He was a self-taught lawyer, a state senator, a superior court judge, and a judge in Connecticut for fourteen years. He was a member of the Continental Congress and helped draft the Declaration of Independence. He was a member of the Constitutional Convention, where he made 138 speeches. He was a U.S. Representative, 1789-91, and at the age of 70, was elected a U.S. Senator, 1791-93.

On Thursday, June 28, 1787, during an almost fatal crisis in the Constitutional Convention, Roger Sherman seconded a motion to enact Dr. Benjamin Franklin's request that Congress be opened with prayer each day.[29] This practice has continued since. The heated dispute was over how Congress would insure that the smaller states would be equally represented in comparison with the larger states.

This debate grew so serious that it threatened the convention itself, as some delegates had already left. Shortly after Franklin's call for prayer, Roger Sherman made the suggestion that state representation in the Senate be equal and that state representation in the House be based on population. This historic proposal, which came to be called the "Connecticut Compromise," was adopted and the system has been in use since. Roger Sherman was also on the committee which decided the wording of the First Amendment. He was originally opposed to the First Amendment, considering it unnecessary, since Congress had no authority delegated from the Constitution in such matters.[30]

While he was in Congress, Roger Sherman objected to a report from the War Committee which would have allowed the army to give five hundred lashes by the courts-martial to a delinquent soldier.

So strong was this leading statesman's belief in biblical methods that he successfully opposed the proposal, using for his argument the scripture Deuteronomy chapter 25, verse 3:
Forty stripes he may give him, and not exceed: lest, if he should exceed, and beat him above these with many stripes, then thy brother should seem vile unto thee. [31]

Roger Sherman described the necessity of:
Admiring and thankfully acknowledging the riches of redeeming love, and earnestly imploring that divine assistance which may enable us to live no more to ourselves, but to him who loved us and gave himself to die for us.[32]

Benjamin Rush, also a signer of the Declaration of Independence, wrote his estimation of Roger Sherman in 1777:

He was not less distinguished for his piety than his patriotism. He once objected to a motion for Congress sitting on a Sunday upon an occasion which he thought did not require it, and gave as a reason for his objection a regard for the commands of his Maker.[33]

Why is it that such a giant of a man is so little covered by the textbooks of today? Could it be perhaps that his faith was so indivisible from whom he was that it might be nearly impossible to say much about him without referencing his constant recognition of Almighty God in the affairs of men? To think, the only man to sign all four of our major founding documents, establish prayer in Congress, develop the compromise for just representation between house and senate, and yet nary a schoolchild, nor most Americans for that matter, could name him!

Of all our founding fathers, Roger Sherman had perhaps the most visible witness to his faith, and was highly esteemed by his colleagues and even opponents.

Daniel Defoe was an English author who was one of the originators of the English novel. A merchant by profession, he began writing pamphlets against the Anglican High Church, for which he was fined and placed in stocks. Being nearly 60 years of age, Daniel Defoe began writing novels, the most popular of which were: Robinson Crusoe, 1719; Moll Flanders, 1722, and A Journal of the Plague Year, 1722.

In volume III of A Selection from the Works of Daniel Defoe, he wrote:

In what glorious colors do the Scriptures, upon all occasions, represent these two hand-in-hand graces, faith and repentance? There is not one

mention of faith in the whole Scriptures but what is recommended in some way or other to our admiration, and to our practice; it is the foundation and the top-stone of all religion, the right hand to lead, and the left hand to support, in the whole journey of the Christian, even through this world, and into the next;

in a word, it is the sum and substance of the Gospel foundation.[34].

How incongruous is it to the decoration of the government, that a man should be punished for drunkenness and set in stocks for swearing, but shall have liberty to deny the God of Heaven, and dispute against the very sum and substance of the Christian doctrine; shall banter the Scripture, and make ballads of the Pentateuch; turn all the principles of religion, the salvation of the soul, the death of our Savior, and the revelation of the Gospel into ridicule.

And shall we pretend to reformation of manners, and suppressing immoralities, while such as this is the general mixture of conversation?
If a man talk against the government, or speak scurrilously of the King, he is led to the old Bailey, and from thence to the pillory, or whipping-post, and it should be so; but he may speak treason against the Majesty of Heaven, deny the Godhead of the Redeemer, and make a jest of the Holy Ghost, and thus affront the Power we all adore, and yet with impunity. [35]

James Logan (October 20, 1674-October 31, 1751) was the Chief Justice of the Supreme Court of Pennsylvania, 1731-39, and private Secretary of William Penn. He stated:

Remember thou art by profession a Christian; that is, one who art called after the immaculate Lamb of God, who, by offering Himself a sacrifice

for thee, atoned for thy sins....Rouse with the more simple servants of nature, and borrowing one hour from the sleep of sluggards, spend it in thy chamber in dressing thy soul with prayer and meditation, reading the Scriptures.... Remember that the same enemy that caused thy first parents to forfeit their blessed condition, notwithstanding the gate is now open for restoration, is perpetually using his whole endeavors to prevent thee from attaining this, and frustrate to thee the passion of thy Redeemer. [36]

Jonathan Trumbull (October 12, 1710-August 17, 1785) was a jurist, clergyman, businessman and the British Governor of Connecticut, appointed by King George III. He was also the father of the Revolutionary artist of the same name, (1756-1843). He was a close friend of George Washington and a strong supporter of American Independence, contributing large amounts of arms, munitions, supplies, etc.

On October 12, 1770, a Proclamation was given from New Haven by the Honorable Jonathan Trumbull, Esq., Governor of the English Colony of Connecticut, in New England:

Pray that God would graciously pour out His Spirit upon us and make the blessed Gospel in His hand effectual to a thorough reformation and general revival of the holy and peaceful religion of Jesus Christ. [37]

Another Proclamation by His Excellency Jonathan Trumbull, Esq., Governor and Commander in Chief in and over the State of Connecticut, stated:

And I do hereby call upon the people...[to] offer to our Almighty and all-gracious God, through our Great Mediator, our sincere and solemn

prayers for His Divine assistance and the influences of His Holy Spirit. [38]

The words of the honorable jurists of our country's early days found in this chapter are not the wavering, hesitant, insecure words of somewhat committed Sunday-only Christians. When we speak of the Faith of our Founding Fathers, one could hardly dispute that most of the influential minds in our judicial system, rooted in true justice, were unashamed of the Gospel of the Lord Jesus Christ, and recognized, honored and fought for the place of the Word of God in America's court systems.

---

[1] Pennsylvania, Great Law of. December 7, 1682. Benjamin Franklin Morris, The Christian Life and Character of the Civil Institutions of the United States, Developed in the Official and Historical Annals of the Republic (Philadelphia, PA: George W. Childs, 1864), p. 83. "Frame of Government." Charter to William Penn..., and Duke of Yorke's Book of Laws. Remember William Penn, 1644-1944, Tercentenary Memorial (Harrisburg, PA: The Commonwealth of Pennsylvania and Pennsylvania Historical Commission, 1944), p. 85-86. Gary DeMar, God and Government - A Biblical and Historical Study (Atlanta, GA: American Vision Press, 1982), p. 115. "Our Christian Heritage," Letter from Plymouth Rock (Marlborough, NH: The Plymouth Rock Foundation), p. 2. D.P. Diffine, Ph.D., One Nation Under God - How Close a Separation? (Searcy, Arkansas: Harding University, Belden Center for Private Enterprise Education, 6th edition, 1992), p. 4. Gary DeMar, America's Christian History: The Untold Story (Atlanta, GA: American Vision Publishers, Inc., 1993), p. 67. Gary DeMar, "God and the Constitution" (Atlanta, GA: The Biblical Worldview, An American Vision Publication - American Vision, Inc., December 1993), p. 9.

[2] Pennsylvania, Great Law of. December 7, 1682. Charter of William Penn, and Laws of the Province of Pennsylvania, passed between the Years 1682 and 1700 (Harrisberg: 1870), pp. 16-18. Anson Phelps Stokes and Leo Pfeffer, Church and State in the United States (NY: Harper and Row, Publishers, 1950, revised one-volume edition, 1964) p. 19.

[3] Grotius, Hugo. James Madison, Examination of the British Doctrine, 1806. Verna M. Hall, Christian History of the Constitution of the United States of America: Christian Self-Government (San Francisco: Foundation for American Christian Education, 1966, 1980), p. 250. John Eidsmoe, Christianity and the Constitution - The Faith of Our Founding Fathers (Grand Rapids, MI: Baker Book House, A Mott Media Book, 1987; 6th printing, 1993), p. 62.

[4] Grotius, Hugo. 1625. Hugo Grotius, The Rights of War and Peace, (Amsterdam, 1933), 1:4.1.3. William Vasilio Sotirovich, Grotius' Universe: Divine Law and a Quest for Harmony (New York: Vantage Press, 1978), p. 51. John Eidsmoe, Christianity and the Constitution - The Faith of Our Founding Fathers (Grand Rapids, MI: Baker Book House, A Mott Media Book, 1987; 6th printing, 1993), p. 63

[5] Grotius, Hugo. 1625. Hugo Grotius, The Rights of War and Peace. Verna M. Hall, Christian History of the Constitution of the United States of America - Christian Self-Government with Union (San Francisco: Foundation for American Christian Education, 1962, 1979), p. 251. John Eidsmoe, Christianity and the Constitution - The Faith of Our Founding Fathers (Grand Rapids, MI: Baker Book House, A Mott Media Book, 1987; 6th printing, 1993), p. 64.

[6] Grotius, Hugo. 1625. Hugo Grotius, The Rights of War and Peace, II:23:3.4. William Vasilio Sotirovich, Grotius' Universe: Divine Law and a Quest for Harmony (New York: Vantage Press, 1978), p. 58. John Eidsmoe, Christianity and the Constitution - The Faith of Our Founding Fathers (Grand Rapids, MI: Baker Book House, A Mott Media Book, 1987; 6th printing, 1993), p. 64.

[7] Grotius, Hugo. Verna M. Hall and Rosalie J. Slater, Teaching and Learning America's Christian History (San Francisco, CA: Foundation for American Christian Education, 1975), p. 69. Gary DeMar, God and Government-A Biblical and Historical Study (Atlanta, GA: American Vision Press, 1984), p. 12.

[8] Grotius, Hugo. 1625. Hugo Grotius, The Rights of War and Peace, (Amsterdam, 1933), III:25.8. William Vasilio Sotirovich, Grotius' Universe - Divine Law and a Quest for Harmony (New York: Vantage Press, 1978), pp. 7-8. John Eidsmoe, Christianity and the Constitution - The Faith of Our Founding Fathers (Grand Rapids, MI: Baker Book House, A Mott Media Book, 1987; 6th printing, 1993), p. 65.

[9] Grotius, Hugo. Hugo Grotius, Commentary on the Law of Prize and Booty, (Oxford: Clarendon Press, 1950), p. 8. William Vasilio Sotirovich, Grotius' Universe - Divine Law and a Quest for Harmony (New York: Vantage Press, 1978), p. 46. John Eidsmoe, Christianity and the Constitution - The Faith of Our Founding Fathers (Grand Rapids, MI: Baker Book House, A Mott Media Book, 1987, 6th printing 1993), p. 63.

[10] Grotius, Hugo. The Truth of the Christian Religion. Stephen Abbott Northrop, D.D., A Cloud of Witnesses (Portland, OR: American Heritage Ministries, 1987; Mantle Ministries, 228 Still Ridge, Bulverde, Texas), p. 200.

[11] Cotton, John. 1636. Benjamin Fletcher Wright, Jr., American Interpretations of Natural Law (New York: Russell & Russell, 1962), pp. 17-18. John Eidsmoe, Christianity and the Constitution - The Faith of Our Founding Fathers (Grand Rapids, MI: Baker Book House, A Mott Media Book, 1987; 6th printing, 1993), p. 32.

[12] Cotton, John. 1636. Benjamin Fletcher Wright, Jr., American Interpretations of Natural Law (New York: Russell & Russell, 1962), pp. 17-18. John Eidsmoe, Christianity and the Constitution - The Faith of Our Founding Fathers (Grand Rapids, MI: Baker Book House, A Mott Media Book, 1987, 6th printing 1993), p. 32.

[13] Cotton, John. Perry Miller and Thomas H. Johnson, The Puritans: A Sourcebook of Their Writings Vol. I (New York: Harper & Row, 1938, 1963), pp. 212-214. John Eidsmoe, Christianity and the Constitution - The Faith of Our Founding Fathers (Grand Rapids, MI: Baker Book House, A Mott Media Book, 1987; 6th printing, 1993), pp. 34-35.

[14] Cotton, John. Samuel Eliot Morison, "John Winthrop and the Founding of New England," Davis R. B. Ross, Alden T. Vaughan, and John B. Duff, eds., Colonial America: 1607-1763 (New York: Thomas Y. Crowell Co., 1970), p. 25. Peter Marshall and David Manuel, The Light and the Glory (Old Tappan, NJ: Fleming H. Revell, 1977), p. 157. Peter Marshall and David Manuel, The Glory of America (Bloomington, MN: Garborg's Heart 'N Home, Inc., 1991), 12.4.

[15] Hooker, Thomas. Rush H. Limbaugh III, See, I Told You So (New York, NY: reprinted by permission of Pocket Books, a division of Simon & Schuster Inc., 1993), pp. 72-73.

[16] Hooker, Thomas. 1638. Collections of the Connecticut Historical Society, 1:20. Benjamin Fletcher Wright, Jr., American Interpretations of Natural Law (New York: Russell & Russell, 1962), p. 23. John Eidsmoe, Christianity and the Constitution - The Faith of Our Founding Fathers (Grand Rapids, MI: Baker Book House, A Mott Media Book, 1987, 6th printing 1993), p. 35.

[17] Rutherford, Samuel. Samuel Rutherford, Lex, Rex, or The Law and the Prince, 1644 (reprinted Harrisonburg, Virginia: Sprinkle Publications, 1982), pp. 1, 6-7. John Eidsmoe, Christianity and the Constitution - The Faith of Our Founding Fathers (Grand Rapids, MI: Baker Book House, A Mott Media Book, 1987, 6th printing 1993), p. 24.

[18] Rutherford, Samuel. John W. Whitehead, The Second American Revolution (Elgin, IL: Government-A Biblical and Historical Study.David C. Cook, 1982), pp. 30-32. Tim LaHaye, Faith of Our Founding Fathers (Brentwood, TN: Wolgemuth & Hyatt, Publishers, Inc., 1987), pp. 84-88. Gary DeMar, God and (Atlanta, GA: American Vision Press, 1982), p. 99.

[19] Winthrop, John. 1645. Charles Hurd, ed., A Treasury of Great American Speeches (NY: Hawthorne Books, 1959), p. 17.

[20] Locke, John. Donald S. Lutz and Charles S. Hyneman, "The Relative Influence of European Writers on Late Eighteenth-Century American Political Thought," American Political Review 189 (1984): 189-197. (Courtesy of Dr. Wayne House of Dallas Theological Seminary.) John Eidsmoe, Christianity and the Constitution - The Faith of Our Founding Fathers (Grand Rapids, MI: Baker Book House, A Mott Media Book, 1987, 6th printing 1993), pp. 51-53. Stephen K. McDowell and Mark A. Beliles, America's Providential History (Charlottesville, VA: Providence Press, 1988), p. 156. [1760-1805], Origins of American Constitutionalism, (1987).

[21] Locke, John. John Locke, Of Civil Government, Book Two, II:11, III:56; V:25, 55; XVIII:200. John Eidsmoe, Christianity and the Constitution - The Faith of Our Founding Fathers (Grand Rapids, MI: Baker Book House, A Mott Media Book, 1987, 6th printing 1993), p. 61.

[22] Locke, John. August 23, 1689, in his work Of Civil Government. John Locke, The Second Treatise on Civil Government, 1690 (reprinted Buffalo, NY: Prometheus Books, 1986), p. 75. John Locke, Two Treatises on Civil Government (London: George Routledge and Sons, 1903), Book 2, p. 262. Verna M.Hall, The Christian History of the Constitution of the United States of America - Christian Self-Government with Union (San Francisco: Foundation for American Christian Education, 1976), p. 58. Marshall Foster and Mary-Elaine Swanson, The American Covenant - The

Untold Story (Roseburg, OR: Foundation for Christian Self-Government, 1981; Thousand Oaks, CA: The Mayflower Institute, 1983, 1992), p. 108.

[23] Massachusetts, General Court of. 1636. Massachusetts Colonial Records, 1:174. Benjamin Fletcher Wright, Jr., American Interpretations of Natural Law (New York: Russell & Russell, 1962), p. 33. John Eidsmoe, Christianity and the Constitution - The Faith of Our Founding Fathers (Grand Rapids, MI: Baker Book House, A Mott Media Book, 1987, 6th printing 1993), p. 32.

[24] Connecticut, Fundamental Orders (Constitution) of. January 14, 1639. Old South Leaflets, No. 8. John Fiske, The Beginning of New England (Boston: Houghton, Mifflin & Co., 1889, 1898), p. 127-128.

[25] Connecticut, Fundamentals Orders (Constitution) of. January 14, 1639. Old South Leaflets, No. 8.The World Book Encyclopedia, 18 vols. (Chicago, IL: Field Enterprises, Inc., 1957; W.F. Quarrie and Company, 8 vols., 1917; World Book, Inc., 22 vols., 1989), Vol. 3, p. 1675.

[26] Connecticut, Fundamental Orders (Constitution) of. January 14, 1639. John Wingate Thornton, The Pulpit of the American Revolution, 1860 (reprinted NY: Burt Franklin, 1970), p. XIX.

[27] Connecticut, Fundamental Orders (Constitution) of. January 14, 1639, Connecticut Towns of Hartford, Wethersfield, and Windsor. Old South Leaflets, No. 8. Connecticut Colonial Records, Vol. 1, pp. 20-25. Old South Leaflets, Published by the Directors of the Old South Work, Old South Meeting House, Boston, n.d. The Code of 1650, Being a Compilation of the Earliest Laws and Orders of the General Court of Connecticut (Hartford: Silus Andrus, 1822), p. 2. Perley Poore, ed., The Federal and State Constitutions, Colonial Charters, and Other Organic Laws of the United States (Washington, 1877), Part I:249-251. Church of the Holy Trinity v. U.S., 143 U.S. 457, 458, 465-471, 36 L ed 226, (1892), Justice David Josiah Brewer. Charles W. Eliot, LL.D., ed., American Historical Documents 1000-1904 (New York: P.F. Collier & Son Company, The Harvard Classics, 1910), Vol. 43, pp. 63-69. Henry Steele Commager, ed., Documents of American History, 2 vols. (NY: F.S. Crofts and Company, 1934; Appleton-Century-Crofts, Inc., 1948, 6th edition, 1958; Englewood Cliffs, NJ: Prentice Hall, Inc., 9th edition, 1973), Vol. I, pp. 22-23. Paul M. Angle, ed., By These Words (NY: Rand McNally & Company, 1954), pp. 6-7. Verna M. Hall, The Christian History of the Constitution of the United States of America (San Francisco, CA: Foundation for American Christian Education, 1960, 1980), pp. 253-257. The Annals of America, 20 vols. (Chicago, IL: Encyclopedia Britannica, 1968, 1977), Vol. I. p. 157. "Our Christian Heritage," Letter from Plymouth Rock (Marlborough, NH: The Plymouth Rock Foundation), pp. 2, 6. Michael P. Farris, Constitutional Law for Christian Students (Paeonian Springs, VA: Home School Legal Defense Association, 1991), p. 8. Gary DeMar, America's Christian History: The Untold Story (Atlanta, GA: American Vision Publishers, Inc., 1993), p. 37. Stephen McDowell and Mark Beliles, "The Providential Perspective" (Charlottesville, VA: The Providence Foundation, P.O. Box 6759, Charlottesville, Va. 22906, January 1994), Vol. 9, No. 1, p. 1.

[28] Massachusetts Bay Colony, Cambridge Platform of. 1648, included the proposal of William Vassall and others, as recorded in the Plymouth Colony Records IX, 1663. Henry Steele Commager, ed., Documents of American History, 2 vols. (NY: F.S. Crofts and Company, 1934; Appleton-Century-Crofts, Inc., 1948, 6th edition, 1958; Englewood Cliffs, NJ: Prentice Hall, Inc., 9th edition,

1973), Vol. I, pp. 29-31. The Annals of America, 20 vols. (Chicago, IL: Encyclopedia Britannica, 1968), Vol. 1, pp. 90-94.

[29] Sherman, Roger. June 28, 1787. James Madison, Notes of Debates in the Federal Convention of 1787 (1787; reprinted NY: W.W. Norton & Co., 1987), p. 210.

[30] Sherman, Roger. Lewis Henry Boutell, The Life of Roger Sherman (Chicago: A.C. McClure & Co., 1896), p. 213. Tim LaHaye, Faith of Our Founding Fathers (Brentwood, TN: Wolgemuth & Hyatt, Publishers, Inc., 1987), p. 137. Edwin Gaustad, Faith of Our Fathers (San Francisco: Harper & Row, 1987), p. 158.

[31] Sherman, Roger. Christopher Collier, Roger Sherman's Connecticut (Middleton, CT: Wesleyan University Press, 1971), p. 185.

[32] Sherman, Roger. John Eidsmoe, Constitution, p. 321. Peter Marshall and David Manuel, The Glory of America (Bloomington, MN: Garborg's Heart'N Home, Inc., 1991), 8.23.

[33] Sherman, Roger. 1777, comments about Sherman by Benjamin Rush. George W. Corner, ed., Autobiography of Benjamin Rush - His "Travels Through Life" together with His Commonplace Book for 1789-1813 (Princeton, N.J.: Published for The American Philosophical Society by Princeton University Press, 1948), pp. 139-156. Henry Steele Commager, ed., The Great Declaration - A Book for Young Americans (Indianapolis: The Bobbs-Merrill Co., Inc., 1958), p. 26. Henry Steele Commager and Richard B. Morris, eds., The Spirit of 'Seventy-Six (NY: Bobbs-Merrill Co., Inc., 1958, reprinted, NY: Harper & Row, Publishers, 1967), p. 275.

[34] Defoe, Daniel. A Selection from the Works of Daniel Defoe, Vol. III, p. 187. Stephen Abbott Northrop, D.D., A Cloud of Witnesses (Portland, Oregon: American Heritage Ministries, 1987; Mantle Ministries, 228 Still Ridge, Bulverde, Texas), p. 116

[35] Defoe, Daniel. A Selection from the Works of Daniel Defoe, Vol. III, p. 102. Stephen Abbott Northrop, D.D., A Cloud of Witnesses (Portland, Oregon: American Heritage Ministries, 1987; Mantle Ministries, 228 Still Ridge, Bulverde, Texas), pp. 116-117.

[36] Logan, James. Wilson Armstead, Memoirs of James Logan. Stephen Abbott Northrop, D.D., A Cloud of Witnesses (Portland, Oregon: American Heritage Ministries, 1987; Mantle Ministries, 228 Still Ridge, Bulverde, Texas), p. 288-289.

[37] Trumbull, Jonathan. October 12, 1770, A Proclamation given from New Haven by the Honorable Jonathan Trumbull, Esq., Governor of the English Colony of Connecticut, in New England. David Barton, Original Intent (Aledo, TX: Wall Builder Press, 1996), p. 138.

[38] Trumbull, Jonathan. A Proclamation by His Excellency Jonathan Trumbull, Esq., Governor and Commander in Chief in and over the State of Connecticut (Hudson and Goodwin, 1807).

Unwavering Courage:
A Sacred Honor

The risk involved to obtain freedom was the soil in which courage germinated. Driven by a passion for godliness and the dream of free expression of worship, America's settlers were painfully aware of the costs of this great experiment.

As America derived its identity from the dream of liberty, patriotism became the banner of courage. Just as new notions of religious freedom and of justice inspired settlers to take ownership of the American experiment, so patriotism became a badge of courage. The Latin "Amor Patriae", or "love of country" became even more enamoring because America was as much an ideal as it was a defined land mass; its borders were as conceptual as they were geographic, so much so that many who had never traveled took life-threatening journeys to enlist in the political experiment called liberty.

Benjamin Rush would depict American patriotism as requiring a moral duty to conscience and a religious duty to principle in 1773:

Patriotism is as much of virtue as justice, and is as necessary for the support of society as natural affection is for the support of families. The Amor Patriae is both a moral and a religious duty. It comprehends not only the love of our neighbors but of millions of our fellow creatures, not only of the present but of future generations. This virtue we find constitutes a part of the first characters of history. The holy men of old, in proportion to the religious spirit they possessed, were endowed with a public spirit. What did Moses forsake and suffer for his countrymen? What shining examples of patriotism do we behold in Joshua, Samuel and all the illustrious princes, captains and prophets amongst the Jews? St. Paul almost wishes himself accursed for his countrymen and kinsmen after the flesh. Even our savior himself gives a sanction to this virtue. He confined his miracles and gospel at first to his own country.[1]

The founding fathers felt that they were endowed, that is, gifted by God to have the unwavering courage that motivated this sense of patriotism for a nation that had not yet taken structure. That special courage accompanied even the early settlers who came and envisioned a free nation worth risking one's life for.

In 1607, as a result of religious persecution upon their persons, reputations, families and livelihood, the "Separatists," or Pilgrims, departed from England. Governor Bradford recorded:

Being thus constrained to leave their native soyle and countrie, their lands and livings, and all their friends and famillier acquantance...to goe into a countrie they knew not (but by hearsay) where they must learne a new language, and get their livings they knew not how, it being a dear place, and **subject to the miseries of war, it was by many thought an adventure almost desperate, a case intolerable, and a miserie worse than death....**
But these things did not dismay them (though they did sometimes trouble them) for their desires were sett on ye ways of God and to enjoye His ordinances; but they rested in His providence, and knew whom they had believed.[2]

The Pilgrims were indeed set on the fact that they would face opposition. Understanding the risks involved, and their unwavering carriage rested in the disciplines of their faithful walk with Christ.

Edward Winslow was a Pilgrim leader and founder of the Plymouth Colony. Selected as an administrator of the colony, 1621, he served as its English agent from 1629 to 1632. Edward Winslow was Governor of the Plymouth Colony for three separate terms, 1633-34, 1636-37 and 1644-45. He succeeded in developing a friendship with the Indian chief, Massasoit. In October 1646, he returned to England as the agent of Massachusetts Bay, and later served Oliver Cromwell in the English Civil War. His work, Glorious Progress of the Gospel Amongst the Indians in New England, 1646, was instrumental in the formation of the Society for the Propagation of the Gospel in New England.

Edward Winslow who kept detailed records of the Pilgrims' experiences, recounted:

Drought and the like considerations moved not only every good man privately to enter into examination with his own estate between God and his conscience, and so to humiliation before Him, but also to humble ourselves together before the Lord by fasting and prayer.[3]

William Penn (October 14, 1644-July 30, 1718) was the founder of Pennsylvania. He was the son of a British Navy Admiral, of the same name, who discovered Bermuda and helped strengthen the throne of King Charles II. William Penn attended Oxford University, and later studied law.

In 1667, at the age of 22, William Penn was impressed by a sermon delivered by Thomas Loe, entitled, "The Sandy Foundation Shaken." He converted to the Christian beliefs of the Society of Friends, or Quakers, who at that time were scorned and ridiculed.[4]

In his Treatise on the Religion of the Quakers, William Penn proclaimed:

I do declare to the whole world that we believe the Scriptures to contain a declaration of the mind and will of God in and to those ages in which they were written; being given forth by the Holy Ghost moving in the hearts of holy men of God; that they ought also to be read, believed, and fulfilled in our day; being used for reproof and instruction, that the man of God may be perfect. They are a declaration and testimony of heavenly things themselves, and, as such, we carry a high respect for them. We accept them as the words of God Himself.[5]

William Penn became a Quaker preacher and writer. Beginning in 1668, he suffered imprisonment over three times for his faith. Once he was imprisoned in the Tower of London for eight months,[6] during which time he wrote the classic book, *No Cross, No Crown*:

No pain, no palm; no thorns, no throne; no gall, no glory; no cross, no crown.[7] Christ's cross is Christ's way to Christ's crown. This is the subject of the following discourse, first written during my confinement in the Tower of London in the year of 1668, now reprinted with great enlargement of matter and testimonies, that thou mayest be won to Christ, or if won already, brought nearer to Him. It is a path which God in his everlasting kindness guided my feet into, in the flower of my youth, when about two and twenty years of age.
He took me by the hand and led me out of the pleasures, vanities and hopes of the world. I have tasted of Christ's judgements, and of his mercies,

and of the world's frowns and reproaches. I rejoice in my experience, and dedicate it to thy service in Christ....

The unmortified Christian and the heathen are of the same religion, and the deity they truly worship is the god of this world. What shall we eat? What shall we drink? What shall we wear? And how shall we pass away our time? Which way may we gather and perpetuate our names and families in the earth? It is a mournful reflection, but a truth which will not be denied, that these worldly lusts fill up a great part of the study, care and conversation of Christendom.

The false notion that they may be children of God while in a state of disobedience to his holy commandments, and disciples of Jesus though they revolt from his cross, and members of his true church, which is without spot or wrinkle, notwithstanding their lives are full of spots and wrinkles, is of all other deceptions upon themselves the most pernicious to their eternal condition for they are at peace in sin and under a security in their transgression.[8]

William Penn stated:

Read my "No Cross, No Crown." There is instruction. Make your conversation with the most eminent for wisdom and piety, and shun all wicked men as you hope for the blessing of God and the comfort of your father's living and dying prayers. Be sure you speak evil of none, not of the meanest, much less of your superiors as magistrates, guardians, teachers, and elders in Christ.[9]

In 1670, William Penn's father, Sir William Penn, who had been a courageous admiral in the King's navy, died. King Charles II owed him a tremendous amount of money, but being short on funds, decided to repay him with a land grant in America. In 1681, as heir of his father's estate, William Penn received the grant from Charles II. The area consisted of all the land between Maryland and New York. The following year, Penn received from the Duke of York the territory that is now Delaware. William Penn had named the area "Sylvania," meaning "woodland," but King Charles II changed it to "Pennsylvania." The state has since become known as "The Quaker State," due to the members of the Society of Friends who helped found it.[10]

On January 1, 1681, William Penn wrote to a friend concerning the land given to him, declaring he would:

Make and establish such laws as shall best preserve true Christian and civil liberty, in all opposition to all unchristian...practices[11]

I eyed the Lord in obtaining it and more was I drawn inward to look to Him, and to owe it to His hand and power than to any other way. I have so obtained it, and desire to keep it, that I may not be unworthy of His love. God that has given it to me, through many difficulties, will, I believe, bless and make it the seed of a nation[12]

Courageously, William Penn was intent on making friends with the native inhabitants. He insisted on buying parcels of land from the Indians, rather than just taking it. **History records that, due to his fair dealings, the colony never suffered an Indian attack.**[13]

On August 18, 1681, in a letter to the Indians in Pennsylvania, William Penn stated:

My Friends:

There is one great God and Power that hath made the world and all things therein, to whom you and I and all people owe their being and well-being, and to whom you and I must one day give an account, for all that we doe in the world; This great God hath written His law in our hearts by which we are taught and commanded to love and help and doe good to one another and not to doe harm and mischief one unto another....

Now this great God hath pleased to make me concerned in my parts of the world, and the king of the country where I live, hath given unto me a great province therein, but I desire to enjoy it with your love and consent, that we may always live together as neighbors and friends, else what would the great God say to us, who hath made us not to devour and destroy one another, but to live soberly and kindly together in the world....

I have great love and regard towards you, and I desire to gain your love and friendship by a kind, just and peaceable life, and the people I send are of the same mind, and shall in all things behave themselves accordingly....

I shall shortly come to you myself at which time we may more freely and largely confer and discourse of these matters. Receive those presents and tokens which I have sent to you as a testimony to my goodwill to you and my resolution to live justly, peaceably and friendly with you.

I am your loving friend, William Penn.[14]

In 1682, William Penn, who had experienced religious persecution for his faith in England, established the colony as a land of religious freedom, granting toleration to every denomination. He printed advertisements in six different languages and sent them across Europe. Soon Quakers, Mennonites, Lutherans, Dunkards (Church of the Brethren), Moravians, Schwenkfelders, etc., from England, Sweden, Wales, Germany, Scotland and Ireland all began arriving in his "holy experiment." To emphasize his plan for Christians working together, he named their city "Philadelphia," which is Greek for "City of Brotherly Love." His concept was that religion is not to be limited to a Sunday ceremonial ritual, but should be an integral aspect of every day life, demonstrated by working with others. [15]

In 1684, William Penn composed his Prayer for Philadelphia, displayed in the Philadelphia City Hall:

And thou, Philadelphia, the Virgin settlement of this province named before thou wert born, what love, what care, what service and what travail have there been to bring thee forth and preserve thee from such as would abuse and defile thee. O that thou mayest be kept from the evil that would overwhelm thee. That faithful to the God of thy mercies, in the Life of Righteousness, thou mayest be preserved to the end. My soul prays to God for thee, that thou mayest stand in the day of trial, that thy children may be blest of the Lord and thy people saved by His Power.[16]

Penn labored to end slavery in the colonies, established a public grammar school in Philadelphia in 1689, and presented the first plan for a union of the colonies to the Board of Trade in London in 1697. On October 28, 1701, William Penn issued the Charter of Privileges to the province of Pennsylvania. In 1701, William Penn left Pennsylvania for London, unaware that he would never again return to his colony. In his farewell to the inhabitants of Pennsylvania, he stated:

You are come to a quiet land, and liberty and authority are in your hands. Rule for Him under whom the princes of this world will one day esteem it their honor to govern in their places.[17]

In presenting the first proposal for a union of the colonies, Penn had again exhibited his visionary courage, the type of courage that constrained him to challenge world leaders on their philosophies of leadership and rule, such as Peter the Great, Czar of Russia, to whom he wrote:

If thou wouldst rule well, thou must rule for God, and to do that, thou must be ruled by him…Those who will not be governed by God will be ruled by tyrants. [18]

Penn was esteemed because of his foresight and proverbial wisdom often evidenced by his thought-provoking maxims:

True Godliness doesn't turn men out of the World, but enables them to live better in it, and excites their endeavors to mend it.[19]

In his sermon, *A Summons or Call to Christendom - In an earnest expostulation with her to prepare for the Great and Notable Day of the Lord that is at the Door*, William Penn stated:

For in Jesus Christ, the light of the world, are hid all the treasures of wisdom and knowledge; redemption and glory; they are hid from the worldly Christian, from all that are captivated by the spirit and lusts of the world: and whoever would see them (for therein consists the things that belong to their eternal peace) must come to Christ Jesus the true light in their consciences, bring their deeds to Him, love Him and obey Him; whom God hath ordained a light to lighten the Gentiles, and for His salvation to the ends of the earth.

Many considered him to be inspired and his uncanny foresight was deemed by some to be prophetic. Even in his final correspondence, William Penn wrote in a way that characterized him:

My dear Wife and Children:

My love, which neither sea nor land nor death itself can extinguish or lessen toward you, most endearly visits you with eternal embraces, and will

abide with you forever; and may the God of my life watch over you and bless you, and do good in this world and forever!

Some things are upon my spirit to leave with you in your respective capacities, as I am to the one a husband and to the rest a father, if I should never see you more in this world.

My dear wife, remember thou wast the love of my youth and much the joy of my life; the most beloved as well as the most worthy of all my earthly comforts; and the reason of that love was more thy inward than thy outward excellencies, which yet were many.

God knows, and thou knowest it, I can say it was a match of Providence's making and God's image in us both was the first thing, and the most amiable and engaging ornament in our eyes. Now I am to leave thee, and that without knowing whether I shall ever see thee more in this world; take my counsel into thy bosom and let it dwell with thee in my stead while thou livest.

First: Let the fear of the Lord and a zeal and love to his glory dwell richly in thy heart; and thou wilt watch for good over thyself and thy dear children and family, that no rude, light, or bad thing be committed; else God will be offended, and He will repent Himself of the good He intends thee and thine....

And now, my dearest, let me recommend to thy care my dear children; abundantly beloved of me as the Lord's blessings, and the sweet pledges of our mutual and endeared affection. Above all things endeavor to breed them up in the love and virtue, and that holy plain way of it which we have lived in, that the world in no part of it get into my family.

I had rather they were homely than finely bred as to outward behavior; yet I love sweetness mixed with gravity and cheerfulness tempered with sobriety. Religion in the heart leads into this true civility, teaching men and women to be mild and courteous in their behavior, an accomplishment worthy indeed of praise.[20]

The unwavering courage of many of the settlers was motivated by the sacred honor of pursuing the liberty of faith and opportunity that America represented.

Sir William Phips, for example, was a colonial Governor of Massachusetts from 1692-95, who, during the French and Indian Wars, led the troops to capture the French colony of Port Royal. He stated:

I have divers times been in danger of my life; and I have been brought to see that I owe my life to Him who has given His precious life for me. I thank God He has led me to see myself altogether unhappy without an interest in the Lord Jesus Christ, and to close heartily with Him, desiring Him to execute all His offices on my behalf. I have now, for some time, been under serious resolution, that I should avoid whatever I knew to be displeasing to God, that I should serve Him all the days of my life....

I knew that if God had a people anywhere, it was here, and I resolved to rise or fall with them; neglecting very great advantages for my worldly interests, that I might come and enjoy the ordinances of the Lord Jesus here. [21]

Many religious leaders were attracted to this experiment in liberty, and were particularly impressed with the courageous devotion of the entire people of America.

John Wesley was an evangelist and religious leader who founded the Methodist denomination. While students at Oxford University, he and his brother Charles formed a scholarly Christian group called, the "Holy Club." The Wesleys were close friends with George Whitefield, the renowned preacher of the American Great Awakening. In 1738, the Wesleys set sail from England to Georgia to serve as missionaries. During the tumultuous voyage at sea, they observed the faith of the Moravian Christians. There was awakened within them a desire for a more intimate relationship with God, eventually leading them to faith in Christ. Together with George Whitefield, John and Charles Wesley were among the most influential ministers of the 1700's. [22] In his journal, John Wesley wrote:

On shipboard, however, I was again active in outward works: where it pleased God, of his free mercy, to give me twenty-six of the Moravian brethren for companions, who endeavored to shew me a more excellent way.
But I understood it not at first. I was too learned and too wise; so that it seemed foolishness unto me. And I continued...trusting in that righteousness whereby no flesh can be justified.
All the time I was at Savannah I was thus beating the air. Being ignorant of the righteousness of Christ, which, by a living faith in him bringeth salvation to every one that believeth, I sought to establish my own righteousness, and so laboured in the fire all my days.
In my return to England, January 1738, being in imminent danger of death, and very uneasy on that account, I was strongly convinced that the cause of uneasiness

was unbelief, and that the gaining of a true, living faith was the one thing needful for me....

So that when Peter Boehler, whom God prepared for me as soon as I came to London, affirmed of true faith in Christ...that it has those two fruits inseparably attending it, "Dominion over sin, and constant peace, from a sense of forgiveness," I was quite amazed, and looked upon it as a new Gospel....

In the evening, I went very unwillingly to a Society in Aldersgate-Street, where one was reading Luther's preface to the Epistle to the Romans.

About a quarter before nine, while he was describing the change which God works in the heart through faith in Christ, I felt my heart strangely warmed.

I felt I did trust in Christ; Christ alone, for salvation; and an assurance was given me, that he had taken away my sins, even mine, and saved me from the law of sin and death. [23]

This fact of Wesley's personal experience with Christ as a result of his trip to America is not widely known. The unwavering courage in faith of the early Americans rings in the words John Wesley wrote as his Rule:

Do all the good you can,
By all the means you can,
In all the ways you can,
In all the places you can,
At all the times you can,
To all the people you can,
As long as ever you can. [24]

[1] Bennett, William J., ed., The Spirit of America (Touchstone, Simon & Schuster Inc. 1997) p. 41

[2] Bradford, William. 1607, in his work entitled, The History of Plymouth Plantation 1608-1650 (Boston, Massachusetts: Massachusetts Historical Society, 1856; Boston, Massachusetts: Wright and Potter Printing Company, 1898, 1901, from the Original Manuscript, Library of Congress Rare Book Collection, Washington, D.C.; rendered in Modern English, Harold Paget, 1909; NY: Russell and Russell, 1968; NY: Random House, Inc., Modern Library College edition, 1981; San Antonio, TX: American Heritage Classics, Mantle Ministries, 228 Still Ridge, Bulverde, Texas, 1988). Verna M. Hall, comp., Christian History of the Constitution of the United States of America (San Francisco: Foundation for American Christian Education, 1976), p. 186. Marshall Foster and Mary-Elaine Swanson, The American Covenant - The Untold Story (Roseburg, OR: Foundation for Christian Self-Government, 1981; Thousand Oaks, CA: The Mayflower Institute, 1992), p. 32.

[3] Winslow, Edward. Young's Chronicles, p. 350. Peter Marshall and David Manuel, The Glory of America (Bloomington, MN: Garborg's Heart'N Home, Inc., 1991), 10.18.

[4] Penn, William. The World Book Encyclopedia, 18 vols. (Chicago, IL: Field Enterprises, Inc., 1957; W.F. Quarrie and Company, 8 vols., 1917; World Book, Inc., 22 vols., 1989), Vol. 13, pp. 6181-6183, 6192-6195.

[5] Penn, William. Treatise of the Religion of the Quakers. Stephen Abbott Northrop, D.D., A Cloud of Witnesses (Portland, OR: American Heritage Ministries, 1987; Mantle Ministries, 228 Still Ridge, Bulverde, Texas), p. 355.

[6] Penn, William. The World Book Encyclopedia, 18 vols. (Chicago, IL: Field Enterprises, Inc., 1957; W.F. Quarrie and Company, 8 vols., 1917; World Book, Inc., 22 vols., 1989), Vol. 13, pp. 6181-6183, 6192-6195.

[7] Penn, William. No Cross, No Crown, 1668. Burton Stevenson, The Home Book of Quotations (New York: Dodd, Mead and Company, 1967), p. 267.

[8] Penn, William. From his writing No Cross, No Crown, written while imprisoned in the Tower of London for 8 months. Thomas Pyrn Cope, ed., Passages from the Life and Writings of William Penn (Philadelphia: Friends Bookstore, 1882).

[9] Penn, William. Chambers' Cyclopedia of English Literature, Acme Edition, vol.III, p. 12. Stephen Abbott Northrop, D.D., A Cloud of Witnesses (Portland, OR: American Heritage Ministries, 1987; Mantle Ministries, 228 Still Ridge, Bulverde, Texas), p. 355.

[10] Penn, William. The World Book Encyclopedia, 18 vols. (Chicago, IL: Field Enterprises, Inc., 1957; W.F. Quarrie and Company, 8 vols., 1917; World Book, Inc., 22 vols., 1989), Vol. 13, pp. 6181-6183, 6192-6195.

[11] . Penn, William. January 1, 1681. Peter G. Mode, Sourcebook and Bibliographical Guide for American Church History (Menasha, WI: George Banta Publishing Co., 1921), p. 163. Thomas

Clarkson, Memoirs of the Private and Public Life of William Penn (London: Longman, Hunt, Rees, Orme, & Brown, 1813), Vol. I, p. 287.

[12] Penn, William. January 1, 1681. Remember William Penn, 1644-1944, Tercentenary Memorial (Harrisburg, PA: The Commonwealth of Pennsylvania and Pennsylvania Historical Commission, 1944). Thomas Clarkson, Memoirs of the Private and Public Life of William Penn (London: Longman, Hunt, Rees, Orme, & Brown, 1813), Vol. I, p. 280. Robert Flood, The Rebirth of America (Philadelphia: Arthur S. DeMoss Foundation, 1986), pp. 46-47.

[13] Penn, William. The World Book Encyclopedia, 18 vols. (Chicago, IL: Field Enterprises, Inc., 1957; W.F. Quarrie and Company, 8 vols., 1917; World Book, Inc., 22 vols., 1989), Vol. 13, pp. 6181-6183, 6192-6195.

[14] Penn, William. August 18, 1681, in his letter to the Indians before his arrival. Pennsylvania Historical Society Collection, Philadelphia.

[15] Penn, William. The World Book Encyclopedia, 18 vols. (Chicago, IL: Field Enterprises, Inc., 1957; W.F. Quarrie and Company, 8 vols., 1917; World Book, Inc., 22 vols., 1989), Vol. 13, pp. 6181-6183, 6192-6195.

[16] Penn, William. 1684. William Penn, Prayer for Philadelphia (Philadelphia, PA: Historical Society of Pennsylvania).

[17] Penn, William. 1701, in his farewell to the Pennsylvania Colony. George Bancroft, History of the United States of America, 6 vols. (Boston: Charles C. Little and James Brown, Third Edition, 1838), Vol. 2, p. 393. Gary DeMar, "God and the Constitution" (Atlanta, GA: The Biblical Worldview, An American Vision Publication - American Vision, Inc., December 1993), p. 9.

[18] Penn, William. Stephen K. McDowell and Mark A. Beliles, America's Providential History (Charlottesville, VA: Providence Press, 1988), p. 62. Hildegarde Dolson, William Penn: Quaker Hero (NY: Random House, 1961), p. 155. D.P. Diffine, Ph.D., One Nation Under God - How Close a Separation? (Searcy, Arkansas: Harding University, Belden Center for Private Enterprise Education, 6th edition, 1992), p. 4. The Annals of America, 20 vols. (Chicago, IL: Encyclopedia Britannica, 1968), Vol. I, p. 189. Charles Fadiman, ed., The American Treasury (NY: Harper & Brothers, Publishers, 1955), p. 116.

[19] Penn, William. Peter Marshall and David Manuel, The Glory of America (Bloomington, MN: Garborg's Heart 'N Home, Inc., 1991), 10.14.

[20] Penn, William. In a letter to his wife and family. Thomas Pyrn, editor, Passages from the Life and Writings of William Penn (Philadelphia: Friends Bookstore, 1882).

[21] Phipps, Sir William. Lives of the Great Fathers of New England, pp. 240-241. Stephen Abbott Northrop, D.D., A Cloud of Witnesses (Portland, OR: American Heritage Ministries, 1987; Mantle Ministries, 228 Still Ridge, Bulverde, Texas), pp. 359-360.

[22] Wesley, John. Stephen K. McDowell and Mark A. Beliles, America's Providential History (Charlottesville, VA: Providence Press, 1988), p. 55.

[23] Wesley, John. May 24, 1738, Wednesday. John Wesley's Journal (Curnock). "From the Journal" (Carol Stream, IL: Christian History), Vol. II, No. I, pp. 30-32.

[24] Wesley, John. In his Rule. John Bartlett, Bartlett's Familiar Quotations (Boston: Little, Brown and Company, 1855, 1980), p. 346.

The Success of Industry:
Work Improves Everybody's Life

One of the distinctions that made America different during its founding days was the penchant for work or industry that seemed to be a universal value among the settlers. **Part of the miracle that made this new nation so productive was, because of the strong Christian ethic, it seemed that each individual understood his or her specific calling and role to make this new society function at maximum efficiency.**

Certainly survival was a motivator, but more than that, the settlers honored their liberty and freedom to worship, through their work, thereby acknowledging their collaboration with God to prove to the world that this new form of government was indeed God's plan. They worked for the glory of God and for their patriotic sense of community.

The church had, throughout the centuries, regarded trades conducted for profit as being somewhat corrupt by their very nature.

Chuck Colson and Jack Eckerd in <u>Why America Doesn't Work</u> explain this phenomenon articulately:

"Until the Reformation, the churches viewed trade carried on for profit as inherently immoral. But the reformers maintained that all work, including that of the tradesman or businessmen, could be pleasing to God. Business was liberated, providing the essential incentives for the work ethic and thus fueling the great Industrial Revolution of the West."

The feudal establishment was not amused by these radical doctrines which spread like wildfire. In fact one of the charges of heresy against English reformer William Tyndale was that he taught: "If we look externally, there is a difference between the washing of dishes and preaching the Word of God, but as touching to please God, in relation to his call, none at all."

Such teachings freed people to do what they did best for God's glory, and a new breed of workers was born. Out of religious convictions these men and women sought excellence and shunned idleness, vanity and waste as deadly sins.

To ignore the religious roots of the work ethic is to ignore the clear evidence of history. The most precious cargo carried by the shiploads of immigrants who set sail for the new world seeking religious freedom and economic opportunity was their view of work. Primarily Puritans and Quakers, they came as laborers for their Lord, straighteners of crooked places, engaged in a task filled with hardship, deprivation and toil.

Contrary to what is often supposed, the much maligned Puritans did not seek wealth as the ultimate reward, neither did they make the mistake of some modern men and worship work itself. They worshipped God -- -- what cultural critic Os Guinness calls the "audience of one" -- -- through their work, which enabled them to treat success with equanimity and failure without regret.

Nor did the Puritans regard wealth as a badge of piety (as many television preachers do today). Wealth and possessions could be a blessing, a testing or even an abandonment to one's own covetousness. Prosperity could also be evidence of Satanic attack. The Puritans viewed work as stewardship to God, which made their primary rewards spiritual and moral.[1]

"Choose that employment or calling in which you may be most serviceable to God," said Puritan writer Richard Baxter. "Choose not that in which you may be most rich or honorable in the world; but that in which you may do most good, and best escape sinning."

The Puritans came to the new world to demonstrate, as William Penn wrote, "what sobriety and industry can do in the wilderness against heat, cold, wanton dangers." Thus hard work and determination became equated with the moral life, and out of this they fashioned a new land with a new ethic.

As a result, the virtue of work became as deeply ingrained in American culture as democracy. Over succeeding generations this ethic produced a thriving society and later fueled the Industrial Revolution which produced vast increases in invention, productivity, and wealth.[2]

Of the founding Fathers, the one that probably most exemplified success achieved through the opportunity afforded by the free enterprise system was **Ben Franklin**. His work ethic proved that the new world provided the environment for one to become whatever they desired.

He was an American printer, writer, scientist, philosopher and statesman. Born to a poor candle-maker in Boston, Massachusetts, he was the 15th of 17 children. Since his family could not afford to provide him with a formal education, he began apprenticing as a printer at the age of twelve. In 1723, he moved to Philadelphia and married Deborah Read, by whom he had two children. He initially gained literary acclaim through the annual publication of his book, Poor Richard's Almanac (1732-57).

At the age of forty-two he was successful enough to retire and devote himself to science, writing and public life. In 1743, he helped found the American Philosophical Society.

Benjamin Franklin, who had taught himself five languages, became known as "the Newton of his Age."

His experiments in electrostatics that required two years of persistence and diligence showed his work habits, and eventually led to the well-known kite experiment that proved lightning was a form of electricity. His invention of the lightning rod earned him honorary degrees from Harvard and Yale, 1753, and the Royal Society's Copley Medal.

He is credited for having coined the terms "battery," "condenser," "conductor," "positive and negative charges" and "electric shock."

He invented the Franklin stove, the rocking chair, bi-focal glasses and the glass harmonica, in addition to numerous scientific discoveries. He developed theories regarding heat absorption, meteorology and ocean currents.

Benjamin Franklin organized the first postal system in America, serving as the deputy postmaster general of the colonies. He established the first volunteer fire department, a circulating public library, and the lighting of city streets.

He helped found the University of Pennsylvania, a hospital, an insurance company, a city police force, a night watch and in 1747, the first militia. In 1754, he organized defenses in the French and Indian War.

Benjamin Franklin was Pennsylvania's delegate to the Albany Congress and acted as its agent in London. He helped draft and signed the Declaration of Independence.

In 1776, he served as a diplomat to France, and was largely responsible for France joining the Revolutionary War on the side of the Colonies. In 1785, he became the President (Governor) of Pennsylvania and signed the Treaty of Alliance, the Treaty of Peace, the Articles of Confederation, and the United States Constitution. He supported the abolition of slavery and in 1788 he was appointed the first president of the first anti-slavery society in America.

In Poor Richard's Almanac, Benjamin Franklin published proverbs such as:

God heals, and the doctor takes the fees.[3]
God helps them that help themselves.[4]

Work as if you were to live 100 years; pray as if you were to die tomorrow.[5]

Benjamin Franklin once remarked to his wife:
Debby, I wish the good Lord had seen fit to make each day just twice as long as it is. Perhaps then I could really accomplish something.[6]

Regarding prayer, Benjamin Franklin wrote:

Being mindful that before I address the Deity my soul ought to be calm and serene, free from passion and perturbation, or otherwise elevated with rational joy and pleasure, I ought to use a countenance that expresses a filial respect, mixed with a kind of smiling that signifies inward joy and satisfaction and admiration. [7]

Let me not fail, then, to praise my God continually, for it is His due, and it is all I can return for His many favors and great goodness to me; and let me resolve to be virtuous, that I may be happy, that I may please Him, who is delighted to see me happy. Amen! [8]

That I may be preserved from atheism and infidelity, impiety and profaneness, and in my addresses to Thee carefully avoid irreverence and ostentation, formality and odious hypocrisy,
Help me, O Father. [9]

And forasmuch as ingratitude is one of the most odious of vices, let me not be unmindful gratefully to acknowledge the favours I receive from Heaven...for all Thy innumerable benefits; for life and reason, and the use of speech, for health and joy and every pleasant hour, my Good God, I thank Thee. [10]

Many of Benjamin Franklin's axioms are contained in his Maxims and Morals:

Contrary habits must be broken, and good ones acquired and established, before we can have any dependence on a steady, uniform rectitude of conduct.

Freedom is not a gift bestowed upon us by other men, but a right that belongs to us by the laws of God and nature.

Without virtue man can have no happiness.

Virtue alone is sufficient to make a man great, glorious and happy.

Self-denial is really the highest self-gratification.

Hope and faith may be more firmly grounded upon Charity than Charity upon hope and faith.

Beware of little expenses.

I never doubted the existence of the Deity, that he made the world, and governed it by His Providence.

The event God only knows.

Good wives and good plantations are made by good husbands.

Let the fair sex be assured that I shall always treat them and their affairs with the utmost decency and respect.

Virtue is not secure until its practice has become habitual.

Nothing is so likely to make a man's fortune as virtue.

My father convinced me that nothing was useful which was not honest.

The pleasures of this world are rather from God's goodness than our own merit.

Search others for their virtues, thy self for thy vices.

Let no pleasure tempt thee, no profit allure thee, no ambition corrupt thee, no example sway thee, no persuasion move thee to do anything which thou knowest to be evil; so thou shalt live jollily, for a good conscience is a continual Christmas.

Remember Job suffered and was afterwards prosperous.

Keep your eyes open before marriage, half shut afterwards.[11]

While some would attribute the numerous accomplishments to his industry, or workaholism, the fact remains that the remarkable productivity of all of the Founding Fathers was not merely attributable to hard work. The work ethic of these super productive individuals was extraordinary, but the hidden secret was a dedicated and faith-filled prayer life. In true humility they reminded themselves and each other of the dangers of pride when one thinks their success is solely attributable to their own efforts.

In 1757, in an essay entitled The Ways to Wealth, composed while sailing as a Colonial Agent to England, Benjamin Franklin wrote:
This doctrine, my friends, is reason and wisdom; **but after all, do not depend too much upon your own industry**, and frugality, and prudence,

though excellent things, for they may all be blasted without the blessing of Heaven; and therefore, ask that blessing humbly, and be not uncharitable to those that at the present seem to want [lack] it, but comfort and help them. Remember, Job suffered, and was afterwards prosperous. [12]

Almighty God, **the Giver of all good things, without whose help all labor is ineffectual**, and without whose grace all wisdom is folly, grant, I beseech Thee, that in this undertaking Thy Holy Spirit may not be withheld from me, but that I may promote Thy glory and the salvation of myself and others; grant this, O Lord, for the sake of Thy Son, Jesus Christ. [13]

As famous as he was for his exhortations for thrift and industry, Benjamin Franklin never believed that making money was our highest calling. In 1737, Franklin wrote in his Poor Richard's Almanac, "the noblest question in the world is 'What good may I do in it?" And so, in 1740 Franklin applied his industry and skills toward the invention of a more efficient and economical stove. The "Franklin stove," as it became known, made everyday life much more comfortable for thousands of Americans who had, up to this point, put up with deficient heating mechanisms. Soon, nearly all homes in America (including Jefferson's Monticello) were heated by the superior Franklin stove. Franklin was offered a patent giving him sole rights to sell the stove for a fixed period of time, but he opted not to (even though he could've made a vast fortune) so that it could be more widely enjoyed by more Americans.[14]

Franklin arrived in Philadelphia in 1723 with only a few coins in his pocket, in stark contrast to his death as a very wealthy man. At his death in 1790, he held numerous properties in Philadelphia, a home in Boston, pasture lands outside Philadelphia and land in Georgia, Nova Scotia and elsewhere. When he died, his estate was worth over $250,000 -- -- by today's dollars, he was the equivalent of a multimillionaire.

Franklin never forgot the "kind loans" two friends gave him as a young man which, he noted, served as "the foundation of my fortune". To give others a start to their fortune -- -- "to be useful even after my death if possible", as he put it in his will -- -- he bequeathed trust funds of 1,000 pounds each to his hometown of Boston and his adopted town of Philadelphia. Franklin instructed that loans were to be made "to such young married artisiceirs, under the age of 25 years, as have served an apprenticeship in the said town, and faithfully fulfilled the duties required in their indentures, so as to obtain a good moral character from at least two respectable citizens who are willing to become their sureties." Under Franklin's plan, loans would be given to young entrepreneurs at five percent interest. It was his hope that the trust would "be continually augmented by the interest" and would grow over the next 100 years, even 200 years.

Franklin calculated that each fund would be worth 131,000 pounds after 100 years. At which time he instructed that 100,000 pounds of the fund be invested in public works projects, such as roads and bridges, and in Philadelphia by making the Schuylkill River navigable. The remaining 31,000 pounds would continue to be loaned at interest. At the end of 200 years, Franklin stipulated that the sum was to be divided between the town of Boston and the state of Massachusetts; and similarly, between Philadelphia and the state of Pennsylvania. He didn't leave any more explicit instructions, "not presuming to carry my views farther."

In 1990, 200 years after his death, the two trust funds were worth $6.5 million. Some of this money was designated as grants to help young people learn a trade or craft, young people today who, like Franklin in 1723, are eager to make good in life.[15]

---

[1] Colson, Charles and Eckerd, Jack, Why America Doesn't Work, (Word Publishing, Dallas, TX, 1991)
pp. 37-38

[2] Colson, Charles and Eckerd, Jack, Why America Doesn't Work, (Word Publishing, Dallas, TX, 1991)
pp. 38-39

[3] Franklin, Benjamin. Poor Richard's Almanac. Carroll E. Simcox, comp., 4400 Quotations for Christian Communicators (Grand Rapids, MI: Baker Book House, 1991), p. 185.

[4] Franklin, Benjamin. 1733, in Poor Richard's Almanac. Raymond A. St. John, American Literature for Christian Schools (Greenville, SC: Bob Jones University Press, Inc., 1979), p. 126. John Bartlett, Bartlett's Familiar Quotations (Boston: Little, Brown and Company, 1855, 1980), p. 347.

[5] Franklin, Benjamin. May 1757, in Poor Richard's Almanac. Carroll E. Simcox, comp., 4400 Quotations for Christian Communicators (Grand Rapids, MI: Baker Book House, 1991), p. 297. John Bartlett, Bartlett's Familiar Quotations (Boston: Little, Brown and Company, 1855, 1980), p. 347.

[6] Franklin, Benjamin. In a comment to his wife. The World Book Encyclopedia, 18 vols. (Chicago, IL: Field Enterprises, Inc., 1957; W.F. Quarrie and Company, 8 vols., 1917; World Book, Inc., 22 vols., 1989), Vol. 6, p. 2748.

[7] Franklin, Benjamin. Carl Becker, Benjamin Franklin (New York: Cornell University, 1946), p. 81. Tim LaHaye, Faith of Our Founding Fathers (Brentwood, TN: Wolgemuth & Hyatt, Publishers, Inc., 1987),
p. 122.

[8] Franklin, Benjamin. 1728, in his "Articles of Belief and Acts of Religion." Jared Sparks, ed., The Writings of Benjamin Franklin (Boston: Tappan, Whittemore and Mason, 1840), Vol. II, pp. 1-3. The Annals of America, 20 vols. (Chicago, IL: Encyclopedia Britannica, 1968), Vol. 1 pp. 373-74.

[9] Franklin, Benjamin. Leonard Labaree, ed., The Papers of Benjamin Franklin (New Haven: Yale University Press, 1959), Vol. I, p. 108. Tim LaHaye, Faith of Our Founding Fathers (Brentwood, TN: Wolgemuth & Hyatt, Publishers, Inc., 1987), p. 120.

[10] Franklin, Benjamin. Leonard Labaree, ed., The Papers of Benjamin Franklin (New Haven: Yale University Press, 1959), Vol. I, p. 109. Tim LaHaye, Faith of Our Founding Fathers (Brentwood, TN: Wolgemuth & Hyatt, Publishers, Inc., 1987), p. 120.

[11] Franklin, Benjamin. William S. Pfaff, ed., Maxims and Morals of Benjamin Franklin (New Orleans: Searcy and Pfaff, Ltd., 1927).

[12] Franklin, Benjamin. 1757, in The Way to Wealth. Raymond A. St. John, American Literature for Christian Schools (Greenville, SC: Bob Jones University Press, Inc., 1979), p. 128.

[13] Johnson, Samuel. Prayer before Writing The Rambler. Stephen Abbott Northrop, D.D., A Cloud of Witnesses (Portland, OR: American Heritage Ministries, 1987; Mantle Ministries, 228 Still Ridge, Bulverde, Texas), p. 256.

[14] Bennett, William J., ed., The Spirit of America (Touchstone, Simon & Schuster Inc. 1997), p.297.

[15] Bennett, William J., ed., The Spirit of America (Touchstone, Simon & Schuster Inc. 1997), pp. 308-309.

The Learned Life:
Inspired Understanding

Large numbers of young Americans have not been informed that America's leading institutions of higher learning were founded as faith-based institutions. Not surprisingly, the Founding Fathers felt that all education ought to be faith-based and that education would develop the heart and character issues, in addition to informing the mind.

William Bennett described the mind-set this way:
Any "general diffusion of knowledge," as Jefferson called it, would be necessary to turn Americans into informed, responsible citizens, or, in the words of Benjamin Roche, into "republican (note: small r) machines".

There were several reasons for promoting a general diffusion of knowledge. First was the creation of a "natural aristocracy," as Jefferson put it, of genius and virtue. This would be no aristocracy of wealth, caste, or privilege. Because genius and virtue are not limited to any particular class, but scattered randomly throughout the Publick, Jefferson's reform of education would reach out to all Americans -- -- the goal being to separate that "best genius... from the rubbish annually." Jefferson was not want to mince words, but his goal was an admirable one. All children, no matter what their background, were to be given an opportunity to rise to their potential. By separating the "wheat from the chaff," as Jefferson biblically referred, he hoped to elevate worthy persons to guard the sacred rights of liberty.

However, Jefferson and the other founders were not content to rely simply on an aristoi or "elite" -- -- no matter how natural -- -- to safeguard the republic from tyranny. This was a democracy after all. As students of the histories of republics, the founders knew all too well the tendency of republics to devolve into oligarchies or tyrannies. Schools provided the "best security against crafty and dangerous encroachments on the public liberty," observed James Madison.

However, more was at stake in checking would-be tyrants. Character formation was also the business of educators. This meant that not only should teachers educate the "abilities" of children but also, and more important, according to Noah Webster, their "hearts" as well. Samuel Adams described the mission of educators as keeping alive the "moral sense" of children. "Great learning and superior abilities, should you ever possess some," Abigail Adams told John Quincy, "will be of little value and small estimation, unless virtue, honor, truth and integrity are added to them."

But still more was to be asked of education. In addition to planting virtues in the heart, and cultivating Jefferson's "natural aristocracy," an education should harvest patriots. It must encourage children to love their country and to be useful citizens. The founders believed that what was needed was a civic education, one that shaped both minds and hearts to prepare Americans for the requirements of self-government. This civic mission of education was regarded as fundamental to the future prosperity of America. Children would learn to revere their laws and to become acquainted with the heroes and ideas of their collective past. This education begins in the home and is carried on in the schools. As Noah Webster put it, as soon as a child "opens his lips...he should list the praise of liberty and of those illustrious heroes" of our founding; Washington wrote that children should learn reverence for laws. [1a]

John Harvard was the first benefactor of Harvard College. Born in London, he imigrated to Massachusetts, 1637 and served as Charlestown's minister. He bequeathed his library and half of his estate for the founding of the first college in America, which was subsequently named in his honor. In 1639, the following was recorded in the Old South Leaflets:

After God had carried us safe to New-England, and wee had builded our houses, provided necessaries for our livelihood, rear'd convenient places for God's worship, and settled the Civill Government: One of the next things we longed for, and looked after was to advance Learning and to perpetuate it to Posterity; **dreading to leave an illiterate Ministry to the Churches, when our present Ministers shall lie in the Dust.** And as wee were thinking and consulting how to effect this great Work, **it pleased God to stir up the heart of one Mr. Harvard, a godly gentleman and a lover of learning there living amongst us**, to give the one half of his estate...towards the erecting of a college and all his Library...[1]

And so it was that Harvard University (1636), was founded by the General Court of Massachusetts only sixteen years after the landing of the Pilgrims, and is the oldest university in the United States. Originally called the College at Cambridge, being established in Cambridge, Massachusetts, it was renamed after its first major benefactor, Rev. John Harvard. The declared purpose of the college was:

To train a literate clergy. [2]

The Rules and Precepts observed at Harvard, September 26, 1642, stated:

1. When any Scholar...is able to make and speak true Latine in Verse and Prose...And decline perfectly the paradigims of Nounes and Verbes in the Greek tongue...[he is able] of admission into the college.

2. Let every Student be plainly instructed, and earnestly pressed to consider well, the maine end of his life and studies is, to know God and Jesus Christ which is eternall life, John 17:3 and therefore to lay Christ in the bottome, as the only foundation of all sound knowledge and Learning. And seeing the Lord only giveth wisedome, Let every one seriously set himself by prayer in secret to seeke it of him, Proverbs, chapters 2 and 3.

3. Every one shall so exercise himselfe in reading the Scriptures twice a day, that he shall be ready to give such an account of his proficiency therein, both in Theoreticall observations of Language and Logick, and in practicall and spirituall truths, as his Tutor shall require, according to his ability; seeing the entrance of the word giveth light, it giveth understanding to the simple, Psalm, 119:130.

4. That they eshewing all profanation of Gods name, Attributes, Word, Ordinances, and times of Worship, do studie with good conscience carefully to retaine God, and the love of his truth in their mindes, else let them know, that (notwithstanding their Learning) God may give them up to strong delusions, and in the end to a reprobate minde, 2Thes. 2:11, 12. Rom. 1:28.

5. That they studiously redeeme the time; observe the generall houres...diligently attend the Lectures, without any disturbance by word or gesture...

6. None shall...frequent the company and society of such men as lead an unfit, and dissolute life. Nor shall any without his Tutors leave, or without the call of Parents or Guardians, goe abroad to other Townes.

7. Every Scholar shall be present in his Tutors chamber at the 7th houre in the morning, immediately after the sound of the Bell, at his opening the Scripture and prayer, so also at the 5th houre at night, and then give account of his owne private reading...But if any...shall absent himself from prayer or Lectures, he shall bee lyable to Admonition, if he offend above once a weeke.

8. If any Scholar shall be found to transgresse any of the Lawes of God, or the Schoole...he may bee admonished at the publick monethly Act.[3]

This author must again resist the temptation for commentary here, or perhaps that will be another book. Trying to stay true to the mission of this work, i.e., helping the reader draw their conclusions as convicted to do so by the words of our forefathers, suffice it to say that today these institutions are a far cry from these original intentions.

Ten of the twelve presidents of Harvard, prior to the Revolutionary War, were ministers,[4] and according to reliable calculations, over fifty percent of the seventeenth-century Harvard graduates became ministers.[5] It should be noted that 106 of the first 108 schools in America were founded on the Christian faith.[6]

Harvard college was founded in "Christi Gloriam" and later dedicated "Christo et Ecclesiae". The founders of Harvard believed that:

All knowledge without Christ was vain.[7]

The word Veritas, on the college seal, means divine truth.[8] The motto of Harvard was officially:

For Christ and the Church.[9]

On Election Day, May 31, 1775, Harvard President Samuel Langdon addressed the Massachusetts Provincial Congress. The message had a profound impact, resulting in it being published and distributed throughout the colonies:

We have rebelled against God. We have lost the true spirit of Christianity, though we retain the outward profession and form of it. We have neglected and set light by the glorious Gospel of our Lord Jesus Christ and His holy commands and institutions.

The worship of many is but mere compliment to the Deity, while their hearts are far from Him. By many, the Gospel is corrupted into a superficial system of moral philosophy, little better than ancient Platonism...

My brethren, let us repent and implore the divine mercy. Let us amend our ways and our doings, reform everything that has been provoking the Most High, and thus endeavor to obtain the gracious interpositions of providence for our deliverance...

May the Lord hear us in this day of trouble...We will rejoice in His salvation, and in the name of our God, we will set up our banners!...

Wherefore is all this evil upon us? Is it not because we have forsaken the Lord? Can we say we are innocent of crimes against God? No, surely it becomes us to humble ourselves under His mighty hand, that He may exalt us in due time...

My brethren, let us repent and implore the divine mercy. Let us amend our ways and our doings, reform everything that has been provoking the Most High, and thus endeavor to obtain the gracious interpositions of Providence for our deliverance...

If God be for us, who can be against us? The enemy has reproached us for calling on His name and professing our trust in Him. They have made a mock of our solemn fasts and every appearance of serious Christianity in the land... May our land be purged from all its sins! Then the Lord will be our refuge and our strength, a very present help in trouble, and we will have no reason to be afraid, though thousands of enemies set themselves against us round about. May the Lord hear us in this day of trouble...We will rejoice in His salvation, and in the name of our God, we will set up our banners.[10]

The College of William and Mary (1692), was named for King William III, Prince of Orange (1650-1702) and Queen Mary II (1662-1694), who jointly ruled England after James II was driven out. The second oldest college in the United States, it was founded in Williamsburg, Virginia, through the efforts of Reverend James Blair (1656-1743), who was its first president, 1693-1743.

He was president of the Virginia Council and acting governor of the Colony of Virginia, 1740-41. James Blair served as minister of Bruton Parish Church in Williamsburg, 1710-43, and published Our Saviour's Divine Sermon on the Mount, 1722.

In 1749, George Washington received his surveyor's commission from the College of William and Mary, and from 1788 to 1799, served as the College's Chancellor. Benjamin Franklin received an honorary Master of Arts degree from the

College in 1756. In 1782, the College bestowed Thomas Jefferson with a Doctor of Civil Law degree under George Wythe. Notable College of William and Mary alumni include: President James Monroe, President John Tyler, Chief Justice John Marshall and Peyton Randolph, who was the first president of the Continental Congress, as well as sixteen other members of the Continental Congress.[11]

The Charter of the College of William and Mary, granted to James Blair, 1692, stated: William and Mary, by the grace of God, of England, Scotland, France and Ireland, King and Queen, Defenders of the Faith, to all whom these our present Letters shall come, greeting. Forasmuch as our well-beloved and trusty Subjects, constituting the General Assembly of our Colony of Virginia, have had it in their minds, and have proposed to themselves, **to the end that the Church of Virginia may be furnished with a Seminary of Ministers of the Gospel; And that the Youth may be piously educated in Good Letters and Manners, and that the Christian Faith may be propagated amongst the Western Indians, to the glory of God.**[12]

Yale College (1701) was founded by ten Congregational ministers as the Collegiate School at Killingworth, Milford and Saybrook, Connecticut.[13] In 1716, it was moved to New Haven, Connecticut, and in 1718, it was renamed Yale College, after the benefactor Elihu Yale. The act authorizing the new college, passed by the General Court, declared it was to be an institution in which:

Youth may be instructed in the Arts and Sciences who through the blessing of Almighty God may be fitted for Publick employment both in Church and Civil State.[14]

The rules of Yale College, set by the founders, stated:
Whereunto the Liberal, and Religious Education of Suitable youth is under ye blessing of God, a chief, & most probable expedient...we agree to...these Rules:

1. The said rector shall take Especial Care as of the moral Behaviour of the Students at all Times so with industry to and Ground Them well in Theoretical divinity...and [not to] allow them to be Instructed and Grounded in any other Systems or Synopses...To recite the Assemblies Catechism in Latin...[and] such Explanations as may be (through the Blessing of God) most Conducive to their Establishment in the Principles of the Christian protestant Religion.

2. That the said Rector shall Cause the Scriptures Daily...morning and evening to be read by the Students at the times of prayer in the School...Expound practical Theology...Repeat Sermons...studiously Indeavor[ing] in the Education of said students to promote the power and the Purity of Religion and Best Edification and peace of these New England Churches.[15]

The prevailing thought was that an education devoid of developing an understanding and hunger for spiritual things was not really an education at all.

The founders of Yale College stated:
Every student shall consider the main end of his study to wit to know God in Jesus Christ and answerably to lead a Godly, sober life. [16]

In 1755, students of Yale College were instructed:

Above all have an eye to the great end of all your studies, which is to obtain the clearest conceptions of Divine things and to lead you to a saving knowledge of God in his Son Jesus Christ. [17]

Princeton University (1746) was originally called "The College of New Jersey." It was founded in Princeton, New Jersey, by the Presbyterian Church. Many influential individuals served as its president, including: Jonathan Dickinson, Aaron Burr Sr., Jonathan Edwards, Samuel Davies, Samuel Finley and **Woodrow Wilson, who was its first president not a clergyman.**[18] Its president just prior to the Revolutionary War was John Witherspoon, the only clergyman to sign the Declaration of Independence, 1776.

Princeton University, under President John Witherspoon, 1768-94, graduated 478 students who directly shaped America, including: James Madison, who served eight years as Secretary of State and eight years as U.S. President; Aaron Burr, Jr., who was a U.S. Vice-President; 3 U.S. Supreme Court justices; 10 Cabinet members; 13 state governors; 21 U.S. Senators; 39 U.S. Representatives; and 114 ministers.[19] Nine of the 55 delegates to the Constitutional Convention were graduates, including: Gunning Bedford Jr., Del.; David Brearley, N.J.; William Richardson Davie N.C.; Jonathan Dayton, N.J.; William Churchill Houston, N.J.; James Madison, Va.; Alexander Martin, N.C.; Luther Martin, Md.; and William Paterson, N.J.[20]

Princeton University's official motto was:
Under God's Power She Flourishes.[21]

The first president of Princeton University, the Rev. Jonathan Dickinson, stated:

Cursed be all that learning that is contrary to the cross of Christ.[22]

Jonathan Edwards was an American theologian and minister of the Calvinist Puritan tradition. His preaching began the Great Awakening Revival that swept the Colonies. This was responsible in part for uniting the Colonies prior to the Revolutionary War. In 1757, he became the third president of Princeton University. His most notable works include Religious Affections, 1746, and The Freedom of the Will, 1754.

In 1727, he married Sarah Pierrepont. Their success as parents was revealed in a study done in 1900. It showed their descendants included: a dean of a prestigious law school, 1 Vice-President of the United States; 1 comptroller of the U.S. Treasury; 3 U.S. Senators, 3 governors, 3 mayors of large cities, 13 college presidents, 30 judges, 65 professors, 80 public office holders, 100 lawyers and nearly 100 missionaries.[23]

The Colony of Connecticut (1647), passed the School Law of Connecticut, similar to the Old Deluder Satan Law passed in the Colony of Massachusetts, 1642. This law helped to prevent illiteracy, as well as the abuse of power over a population ignorant of Scriptures, as had been the case in Europe. The law stated:

It being one chiefe project of that old deluder, Satan, to keepe men from the knowledge of the Scriptures, as in former time, and that learning may not be buried in the grave of our forefathers in church and Commonwealth...

It is therefore ordered by this Court...that every township within this jurisdiction, after the Lord hath increased them to the number of fifty howshoulders, shall forthwith appoint one within theire towne, to teach all such children as shall resorte to him, to write and read...and it is further ordered, That where any towne shall increase to the number of one hundred families or howshoulders, they shall sett up a grammar schoole for the university.[24]

In Philadelphia, 1749, Benjamin Franklin stated in his Proposals Relating to the Education of Youth in Pennsylvania:

History will also afford the frequent opportunities of showing the necessity of a public religion, from its usefulness to the public; the advantage of a religious character among private persons; the mischiefs of superstition, etc. and the excellency of the Christian religion above all others, ancient or modern.[25]

On August 23, 1750, from Philadelphia, Benjamin Franklin wrote to Dr. Samuel Johnson (October 14, 1696-January 6, 1772), the first President of King's College (now Columbia University) regarding education:

I think with you, that nothing is of more importance for the public weal, than to form and train up youth in wisdom and virtue...I think also, general virtue is more probably to be expected and obtained from the education of youth, than from the exhortation of adult persons; bad habits and vices of the mind being, like diseases of the body, more easily prevented than cured.
I think, moreover, that talents for the education of youth are the gift of God; and that he on whom they are bestowed, whenever a way is opened for the use of them, is as strongly called as if he heard a voice from heaven.[26]

Noah Webster argued for education, prioritizing character over talent: The *virtues* of men are of more consequence to society than their *abilities*; and for this reason, the *heart* should be cultivated with more assiduity than the *head*.[27]

[1a] Bennett, William J., ed., The Spirit of America (Touchstone, Simon & Schuster Inc. 1997) pp. 218-219

[1] Harvard, John. 1642. Old South Leaflets. Peter Marshall and David Manuel, The Glory of America (Bloomington, MN: Garborg's Heart' N Home, Inc., 1991), 9.28.

[2] Harvard, John. 1636. Tim LaHaye, Faith of Our Founding Fathers (Brentwood, TN: Wolgemuth & Hyatt, Publishers, Inc., 1987), p. 32.

[3] Harvard University. 1636. Old South Leaflets. Benjamin Pierce, A History of Harvard University (Cambridge, MA: Brown, Shattuck, and Company, 1833), Appendix, p. 5. Peter G. Mode, ed., Sourcebook and Biographical Guide for American Church History (Menasha, WI: George Banta Publishing Co., 1921), pp. 74-75. Robert Flood, The Rebirth of America (Philadelphia: Arthur S. DeMoss Foundation, 1986), p. 41. "Our Christian Heritage," Letter from Plymouth Rock (Marlborough, NH: The Plymouth Rock Foundation), p. 2. Pat Robertson, America's Dates With Destiny (Nashville, TN: Thomas Nelson Publishers, 1986), pp. 44-45. Gary DeMar, America's Christian History: The Untold Story (Atlanta, GA: American Vision Publishers, Inc., 1993), p. 40. Rosalie J. Slater, "New England's First Fruits, 1643," Teaching and Learning America's Christian History (San Francisco: Foundation for Christian Education, 1980), p. vii. Stephen McDowell and Mark Beliles, "The Providential Perspective" (Charlottesville, VA: The Providence Foundation, P.O. Box 6759, Charlottesville, Va. 22906, January 1994), Vol. 9, No. 1, p. 3. D.P. Diffine, Ph.D., One Nation Under God - How Close a Separation? (Searcy, Arkansas: Harding University, Belden Center for Private Enterprise Education, 6th edition, 1992), p. 4.

[4] Harvard University. 1636. Stephen K. McDowell and Mark A. Beliles, America's Providential History (Charlottesville, VA: Providence Press, 1988), p. 91.

[5] Harvard University. 1636. Quoted in Nancy Leigh DeMoss, ed., "How Christians Started the Ivy League," The Rebirth of America (Philadelphia, PA: Arthur S. DeMoss Foundation, 1986), p. 41. Peter Gay, A Loss of Mastery: Puritan Historians in Colonial America (Berkeley, CA: University of California Press, 1966), p. 23. Gary DeMar, America's Christian History: The Untold Story (Atlanta, GA: American Vision Publishers, Inc., 1993), p. 41.

[6] Harvard University. 1636. "Our Christian Heritage," Letter from Plymouth Rock (Marlborough, NH: The Plymouth Rock Foundation), p. 2.

[7] Harvard University. 1636. Samuel Eliot Morison, "Harvard Seals and Arms," The Harvard Graduates' Magazine (Manesh, WI: George Barna Publishing Co.), September 1933, p. 8. "Our Christian Heritage," Letter from Plymouth Rock (Marlborough, NH: The Plymouth Rock Foundation), p. 2.

[8] Harvard University. 1636. Samuel Eliot Morison, "Harvard Seals and Arms," The Harvard Graduates' Magazine (Manesh, WI: George Barna Publishing Co.), September 1933, p. 8. "Our Christian Heritage," Letter from Plymouth Rock (Marlborough, NH: The Plymouth Rock Foundation), p. 2.

[9] Harvard University. 1636. Samuel Eliot Morison, "Harvard Seals and Arms," The Harvard Graduates' Magazine (Manesh, WI: George Barna Publishing Co.), September 1933, p. 8.

[10] Harvard University. May 31, 1775, in the Election Day sermon, entitled "The Wall," delivered to the Provincial Congress of Massachusetts by Harvard President Samuel Langdon. A.W. Plumstead, ed., The Wall and the Garden, Selected Massachusetts Election Sermons, 1670-1775 (Minneapolis: University of Minnesota Press, 1968), pp. 364-373. Verna M. Hall, Christian History of the American Revolution - Consider and Ponder (San Francisco: Foundation for American Christian Education, 1976), p. 506. Peter Marshall and David Manuel, The Light and the Glory (Old Tappan, New Jersey: Fleming H. Revell Co., 1977), p. 278. Lucille Johnston, Celebrations of a Nation (Arlington, VA: The Year of Thanksgiving Foundation, 1987), p. 77. Peter Marshall and David Manuel, The Light and the Glory (Old Tappan, NJ: Fleming H. Revell, 1977), pp. 277-278. Peter Marshall and David Manuel, The Glory of America (Bloomington, MN: Garborg's Heart'N Home, Inc., 1991), 6.3.

[11] William and Mary, College of. Mary R.M. Goodwin, Wren Building Interpretative Research Report (Williamsburg, VA: College of William and Mary), p. 7.

[12] William and Mary, College of. 1692, in the Original Charter of the College of William and Mary, Williamsburg, Virginia, granted to James Blair. Rare Book Collection, Swem Library. The Charter and Statutes of the College of William and Mary in Virginia (Williamsburg, VA: William Parks, 1736), p. 3. John Fiske, The Beginnings of New England (Boston: Houghton, Mifflin & Co., 1898), pp. 127-128, 136. Russ Walton, Biblical Principles of Importance to Godly Christians (NH: Plymouth Rock Foundation, 1984), p. 356.

[13] Yale College. 1701, founded by ten Congregational ministers. Noah Webster, Letters to a Young Gentleman Commencing His Education (New Haven: Howe & Spalding, 1823), p. 237.

[14] Yale College. 1701, in an act by the General Court. David A. Lockmiller, Scholars on Parade: Colleges, Universities, Costumes and Degrees (New York: MacMillan, 1969), p. 70. Pat Robertson, America's Dates With Destiny (Nashville, TN: Thomas Nelson Publishers, 1986), p. 46. Yale College was renamed Yale University in 1887. The New American Desk Encyclopedia (New York, NY: Signet, The Penguin Group, 1989), p. 1360.

[15] Yale College. November 11, 1701, Proceedings of the Trustees. Franklin B. Dexter, editor, Documentary History of Yale University (New Haven: Yale University Press, 1916; NY: Amo Press & The New York Times, 1969), p. 32. Pat Robertson, America's Dates With Destiny (Nashville, TN: Thomas Nelson Publishers, 1986), pp. 45-46.

[16] Yale College. 1701, as stated by the founders. William C. Ringenberg, The Christian College: A History of Protestant Higher Education in America (Grand Rapids, MI: William B. Eerdmans

Publishing Company, 1984), p. 38. Gary DeMar, America's Christian History: The Untold Story (Atlanta, GA: American Vision Publishers, Inc., 1993), p. 42.

[17] Yale College. 1755, instructions to students, given previously in 1743. The Catalogue of the Library of Yale College in New Haven (New London: T. Green, 1743), prefatory remarks. The Catalogue of the Library of Yale College in New Haven (New Haven: James Parker, 1755), prefatory remarks.

[18] Princeton University. 1746. "(Thomas) Woodrow Wilson, 28th President of the United States, 1913-1921," The World Book Encyclopedia (Chicago, IL: Field Enterprises, Inc., 1957; W.F. Quarrie and Company, 8 vols., 1917; World Book, Inc., 22 vols., 1989), 22 vols.), Vol. 18, p. 8788.

[19] Witherspoon, John. 1768-1794. Martha Lou Lemmon Stohlman, John Witherspoon: Parson, Politician, Patriot (Philadelphia: Westminster Press, 1897), p. 172. John Eidsmoe, Christianity and the Constitution - The Faith of Our Founding Fathers (Grand Rapids, MI: Baker Book House, A Mott Media Book, 1987, 6th printing 1993), p. 83.

[20] Witherspoon, John. 1768-1794. Varnum Lansing Collins, President Witherspoon (New York: Arno Press and The New York Times, 1969), II:229. M.E. Bradford, A Worthy Company (Marlborough, New Hampshire: Plymouth Rock Foundation, 1982). John Eidsmoe, Christianity and the Constitution - The Faith of Our Founding Fathers (Grand Rapids, MI: Baker Book House, A Mott Media Book, 1987, 6th printing 1993), pp. 83, 87. Stephen K. McDowell and Mark A. Beliles, America's Providential History (Charlottesville, VA: Providence Press, 1988), p. 100.

[21] Princeton University. 1746. Stephen K. McDowell and Mark A. Beliles, America's Providential History (Charlottesville, VA: Providence Press, 1988), p. 93.

[22] Princeton University. 1746. Stephen K. McDowell and Mark A. Beliles, America's Providential History (Charlottesville, VA: Providence Press, 1988), p. 93.

[23] Edwards, Jonathan. Marshall Foster, Winning the Battle for the 21st Century (Thousand Oaks, CA: Mayflower Institute, 1993), p. 39.

[24] Connecticut, Colony of. 1647. Old Deluder Satan Law. The Code of 1650 - Being a Compilation of the Earliest Laws and Orders of the General Court of Connecticut (Hartford: Silus Andrus, 1822), pp. 20-91, 92-94. The Laws and Liberties of Massachusetts, 1648 (reprinted Cambridge: 1929), cited in McCollum v. Board of Education, 68 S.Ct. 461, 333 U.S. 203 (1948). Records of the Governor of the Massachusetts Bay in New England, II:203. Church of the Holy Trinity v. United States, 143 US 457, 458, 465-471, 36 L ed 226, Justice David Josiah Brewer. Henry Steele Commager, ed., Documents of American History, 2 vols. (NY: F.S. Crofts and Company, 1934; Appleton-Century-Crofts, Inc., 1948, 6th edition, 1958; Englewood Cliffs, NJ: Prentice Hall, Inc., 9th edition, 1973), Vol. I, p. 29. John Eidsmoe, Christianity and the Constitution - The Faith of Our Founding Fathers (Grand Rapids, MI: Baker Book House, A Mott Media Book, 1987, 6th printing 1993), p. 28. The Annals of America, 20 vols. (Chicago, IL: Encyclopedia Britannica, 1968), Vol. I, p. 203.

[25] Franklin, Benjamin. 1749, in Philadelphia, Proposals Relating to the Education of Youth in Pennsylvania (Philadelphia, 1749), p. 22.

[26] Franklin, Benjamin. August 23, 1750, in a letter to Dr. Samuel Johnson, President of King's College (now Columbia University). Verna M. Hall, The Christian History of the American Revolution (San Francisco: Foundation for Christian Education, 1976), p. 221.

[27] Bennett, William J., ed., The Spirit of America (Touchstone, Simon & Schuster Inc. 1997) p. 267

Faith of Our Founding Fathers:
Opportunity for Revival

An appreciation of where you have come from can sometimes help you appreciate where you should be going. The United States of America exists because some dedicated Christians were passionate enough to commit to trying to establish a free nation, under God. Hopefully, dear reader, you are coming to that conclusion, not because of my words, but because of this collection of their own words.

Today's climate of evident and surrounding moral depravity provides an environment for light to shine in.

Perhaps it will take some committed church communities to emulate some of the virtue of the early American church, which is reminiscent of conditions for the early church at the time of the writing of the New Testament.

Edward Johnson, the founder of Woburn, Massachusetts, was a contemporary of Massachusetts Governor John Winthrop. He became a trader, author, historian, and in 1654, witnessed the founding of the Puritan Church in the New World. Edward Johnson reported this event in his work entitled Wonder-Working Providences of Sion's Saviour in New England:

Although the number of faithful people of Christ were but few, yet their longing desire to gather into a church was very great....

Having fasted and prayed with humble acknowledgment of their own unworthiness to be called of Christ to so worthy a work, they joined together in a holy Covenant with the Lord and with one another, promising by the Lord's assistance to walk together in exhorting, admonishing and rebuking one another, and to cleave to the Lord with a full purpose of heart.

First, it is their judgment, and that from Scripture taught them, that those who are chosen to a place in government, must be men truly fearing God, wise and learned in the truths of Christ...

Neither will any Christian of a sound judgment vote for any, but those who earnestly contend for the faith.[1]

Johnson was fascinated with his friend, then Governor of Massachusetts John Winthrop, who was a catalyst in the spiritual revival that built the population of Massachusetts and New England.

In June of 1630, ten years after the Pilgrims founded the Plymouth Colony, Governor John Winthrop founded the Holy Commonwealth of Massachusetts **with 700 people sailing in eleven ships**. This began the Great Migration, which **saw more than twenty thousand Puritans embark for New England in the pursuing sixteen years**.[2]

Even with our increase in population, it is extremely rare to see twenty thousand people united for a spiritual cause. "Large" churches today lose members when they move a few miles across town, never mind asking their members to sell all and take a life-threatening journey as a group to start all over again.

But persecution will motivate people to go to and grow to great ends for their faith.

Cotton Mather was an American colonial clergyman and educator. He graduated from Harvard, 1678, and joined his father, Increase Mather, in the pastorate of the Second Church in Boston, 1680.

The House of Representatives had attempted to appoint him President of Harvard, 1703. He helped found Yale University, and in 1721, became President of the Connecticut College. He authored 450 books, and was the first person born in America to be elected to the Royal Society of London.

Cotton Mather was regarded as the most brilliant man of New England in his time. Among his many accomplishments was the introduction of the smallpox inoculation during an epidemic in 1721.

In 1702, Cotton Mather published Magnalia Christi Americana (The Great Achievement of Christ in America), which is the most detailed history written of the first 50 years of New England. In it, he stated:

The sum of the matter is that from the beginning of the Reformation in the English nation, there had always been a generation of godly men, desirous to pursue the reformation of religion, according to the Word of God...[though resisted by individuals with] power...in their hands...not only to stop the progress of the desired reformation but also, with innumerable vexation, to persecute those that heartily wish well unto it...[The Puritans were] driven to seek a place for the exercise of the Protestant religion, according to the light of conscience, in the deserts of America.[3]

In observing the rising trend in the Colonies, Cotton Mather wrote: **Religion begat prosperity, and the daughter devoured the mother.** [4]

It is interesting to note that early American Christians regarded the opportunities afforded by a free society as a threat to their virtue, that materialism (or consumerism today) along with power was a dangerous combination, and could only be fended off by strong moral and religious convictions.

William Penn, stated in the preface of the Frame of Government of Pennsylvania:

When the great and wise God had made the world of all His creatures, it pleased him to choose man His deputy to rule it; and to fit him for so great a charge and trust, He did not only qualify him with skill and power but with integrity to use them justly....

The origination and descent of all human power [comes] from God...This settles the divine right of government beyond exception, and that for two ends: first, to terrify evil doers; secondly, to cherish those that do well; which gives government a life beyond corruption, and makes it as durable in the world, as good men shall be.

So that government seems to me a part of religion itself, a thing sacred in its institution and end. For, if it does not directly remove the cause, it crushes the effects of evil, and is as such, (though a lower, yet) an emanation of the same Divine Power, that is both the author and object of pure religion....

Government, like clocks, goes from the motion men give them; and as governments are made and moved by men, so by them they are ruined too.

Wherefore governments rather depend upon men, than men upon governments. Let men be good, and the government cannot be bad...

But if men be bad, let the government be never so good, they will endeavor to warp and spoil it to their turn. I know some say, "Let us have good laws and no matter for the men that execute them." But let them consider that though good laws do well, good men do better, for good laws may want good men and be abolished or invaded by ill men; but good men will never want good laws nor suffer ill ones... **That, therefore, which makes a good constitution must keep it, - namely men of wisdom and virtue, - qualities that, because they descend not with worldly inheritances, must be carefully propagated by a virtuous education of youth....** [Be it enacted] that all persons...having children...shall cause such to be instructed in reading and writing, so that they may be able to read the Scriptures and to write by the time they attain to 12 years of age.[5]

So we have seen that our Founding Fathers felt a moral education was vital to the perpetuation of a free society. But did you, dear reader, realize that the government organizing philosophies calling for the balance of checks and powers between our three branches of government was also a faith-based ideal?

Baron Charles Louis Montesquieu, (January 18, 1689-February 10, 1755), was a French political philosopher who greatly influenced nineteenth century thought. In 1748, he wrote The Spirit of the Laws, introducing a revolutionary concept of government where the powers of a monarch were divided into judicial, legislative and executive bodies to guarantee individual freedoms.

In reviewing nearly 15,000 items written by the Founding Fathers, including newspaper articles, monographs, books, pamphlets, etc., Baron Charles Montesquieu was the most frequently quoted source next to the Bible.[6]

In the beginning of his work The Spirit of the Laws, 1748, Baron Montesquieu wrote:

God is related to the universe, as Creator and Preserver; the laws by which He created all things are those by which He preserves them....

But the intelligent world is far from being so well governed as the physical. For though the former has also its laws, which of their own nature are invariable, it does not conform to them so exactly as the physical world. This is because, on the one hand, particular intelligent beings are of a finite nature, and consequently liable to error; and on the other, their nature requires them to be free agents. Hence they do not steadily conform to their primitive laws; and even those of their own instituting they frequently infringe...

Man, as a physical being, is like other bodies governed by invariable laws. As an intelligent being, he incessantly transgresses the laws established by God, and changes those of his own instituting. He is left to his private direction, though a limited being, and subject, like all finite intelligences, to ignorance and error: even his imperfect knowledge he loses; and as a sensible creature, he is hurried away by a thousand impetuous passions.

Such a being might every instant forget his Creator; God has therefore reminded him of his duty by the laws of religion. Such a being is liable every moment to forget himself; philosophy has provided against this by the laws of morality. Formed to live in society, he might forget his fellow-creatures; legislators have therefore, by political and civil laws, confined him to his duty.[7]

Montesquieu understood the inherently selfish nature of man, and that, opportunity provided, he would accumulate more and more power unto himself, becoming despotic. He based this understanding on Jeremiah 17:9:

The heart is deceitful above all things, and desperately wicked: who can know it? [8]

Montesquieu's philosophy, therefore, promulgated the idea that powers of government should be separated into branches, allowing power to check power in order to safeguard personal liberty. His concept of three branches of Government: Judicial, Legislative and Executive, was based on Isaiah 33:22:

For the Lord is our Judge, the Lord is our lawgiver, the Lord is our king.[9]

In The Spirit of the Laws, Montesquieu wrote:
The Christian religion, which orders men to love one another, no doubt wants the best political laws and the best civil laws for each people, because those laws are, after [religion], the greatest good that men can give and receive.[10]

Nor is there liberty if the power of judging is not separated from legislative power and from executive power. If it [the power of judging] were joined to legislative power, the power over life and liberty of the citizens would be arbitrary, for the judge would be the legislator. If it were joined to executive power, the judge could have the force of an oppressor. All would be lost if the same...body of principal men...exercised these three powers.[11]

It is my contention that a return to understanding the roots of our governmental system can even help create an environment in which spiritual revival is enhanced. America needs to see (and has had periodic glimpses) unusual occurrences that shake communities as in those days.

In his Narrative of Surprising Conversions, Jonathan Edwards wrote:
And then it was, in the latter part of December, that the Spirit of God began extraordinarily to...work amongst us. There were, very suddenly, one after another, five or six persons who were, to all appearance, savingly converted, and some of them wrought upon in a very remarkable manner. Particularly I was surprised with

the relation of a young woman, who had been one of the greatest company-keepers in the whole town. When she came to me, I had never heard that she was become in any ways serious, but by the conversation I had with her, it appeared to me that what she gave an account of was a glorious work of God's infinite power and sovereign grace, and that God had given her a new heart, truly broken and sanctified...

God made it, I suppose, the greatest occasion of awakening to others, of anything that ever came to pass in the town. I have had abundant opportunity to know the effect it had, by my private conversation with many. The news of it seemed to be almost like a flash of lighting upon the hearts of young people all over the town, and upon many others...

Presently upon this, a great and earnest concern about the great things of religion and the eternal world became universal in all parts of the town and among persons of all degrees and all ages. The noise of the dry bones waxed louder and louder... Those that were wont to be the vainest and loosest, and those that had been the most disposed to think and speak slightly of vital and experimental religion, were not generally subject to great awakenings. And the work of conversion was carried on in a most astonishing manner and increased more and more; souls did, as it were, come by flocks to Jesus Christ...

This work of God, as it was carried on and the number of true saints multiplied, soon made a glorious alteration in the town, so that in the spring and summer following, Anno 1735, the town seemed to be full of the presence of God.

It never was so full of love, nor so full of joy...there were remarkable tokens of God's presence in almost every house. It was a time of joy in families on the account of salvation's being brought unto them, parents rejoicing over their children as new born, and husbands over their wives, and wives over their husbands.

The doings of God were then seen in His sanctuary, God's day was a delight and His tabernacles were amiable. Our public assembles were then beautiful; the congregation was alive in God's service, everyone earnestly intent on the public worship, every hearer eager to drink the words of the minister as they came from his mouth. The assembly in general were, from time to time, in tears while the word was preached, some weeping with sorrow and distress, others with joy and love, others with pity and concern for their neighbors.

There were many instances of persons that came from abroad, on visits or on business...[that] partook of that shower of divine blessing that God rained down here and went home rejoicing. Till at length the same work began to appear and prevail in several other towns in the country.

In the month of March, the people of South Hadley began to be seized with a deep concern about the things of religion, which very soon became universal...About the same time, it began to break forth in the west part of Suffield...and it soon spread into all parts of the town. It next appeared at Sunderland...

About the same time it began to appear in a part of Deerfield...Hatfield...West Springfield...Long Meadow...Endfield...Westfield...Northfield...In every place, God brought His saving blessings with Him, and His Word, attended with Spirit...returned not void. [12]

With foresight into our present day struggles with Islam, Montesquieu wrote that the spirit of a Christian revival is best suited for successful government: I have always respected religion; the morality of the Gospel is the noblest gift ever bestowed by God on man. We shall see that we owe to Christianity, in government, a certain political law, and in war a certain law of nations - benefits which human nature can never sufficiently acknowledge.

The principles of Christianity, deeply engraved on the heart, would be infinitely more powerful than the false honor of monarchies, than the humane virtues of republics, or the servile fear of despotic states.

It is the Christian religion that, in spite of the extent of empire and the influence of climate, has hindered despotic power from being established in Ethiopia, and has carried into the heart of Africa the manners and laws of Europe.

The Christian religion is a stranger to mere despotic power. The mildness so frequently recommended in the Gospel is incompatible with the despotic rage with which a prince punishes his subjects, and exercises himself in cruelty...

A moderate Government is most agreeable to the Christian Religion, and a despotic Government to the Mahommedan....While the Mahommedan princes incessantly give or receive death, the religion of the Christians renders their princes less timid, and consequently less cruel.

The prince confides in his subjects, and the subjects in the prince. How admirable the religion which, while it only seems to have in view the felicity of the other life, continues the happiness of this![13]

A spirit of revival will even benefit others in the nation.

In 1754, in a pamphlet entitled Information to Those Who Would Remove to America, Benjamin Franklin wrote to Europeans interested in immigrating or sending their youth to this land:

Hence bad examples to youth are more rare in America, which must be a comfortable consideration to parents. To this may be truly added, that serious religion, under its various denominations, is not only tolerated, but respected and practised.

Atheism is unknown there; Infidelity rare and secret; so that persons may live to a great age in that country without having their piety shocked by meeting with either an Atheist or an Infidel.

And the Divine Being seems to have manifested his approbation of the mutual forbearance and kindness with which the different sects treat each other; by the remarkable prosperity with which he has been pleased to favor the whole country. [14]

Just one year and a couple of months before the signing of the Declaration of Independence, on April 19, 1775, in a Proclamation of a Day of Fasting and Prayer for the Connecticut Colony, Governor Jonathan Trumbull beseeched that: **God would graciously pour out His Holy Spirit on us to bring us to a thorough Repentance and effectual Reformation that our iniquities may not be our ruin; that He would restore, preserve and secure the Liberties of this and all the other British American colonies, and make the Land a mountain of Holiness, and Habitation of Righteousness forever.** [15]

It is both encouraging and exciting to see that a groundswell of prayer and intercession has been churning in the United States that could bring about those same type of revival conditions. In a post-9-11 atmosphere, more and more individuals in the United States are asking spiritual and eternal questions. It is vital for the church (which is made up of dedicated, faithful God-fearing individuals) to be "**ready to always give an answer to those who ask you for the reason for the hope that you have." I Peter 3:15**

The Founding Fathers had a consistent sense of awe about what God was doing in their midst. Benjamin Franklin had become very close friends with George Whitefield, the renowned preacher of the Great Awakening.

In his autobiography, Franklin wrote of having attended the crusades of George Whitefield at the Philadelphia Courthouse steps. He noted over 30,000 people were present, and that Whitefield's voice could be heard nearly a mile away with no amplification. Benjamin Franklin became very appreciative of the preaching of George Whitefield, even to the extent of printing many of his sermons and journals.

So great was the response of the Colonies to Whitefield's preaching of the Gospel, that the churches were not able to hold the people. Benjamin Franklin built a grand auditorium for the sole purpose of having his friend George Whitefield preach in it when he came to Pennsylvania. After the crusades, Franklin donated the auditorium to be the first building of the University of Pennsylvania. A bronze statue of George Whitefield still stands in front, commemorating the Great Awakening Revivals in the colonies prior to the Revolutionary War.

In 1739, noting the effects of George Whitefield's ministry and the resulting Christian influence on city life, Benjamin Franklin later recorded in his autobiography:

It was wonderful to see the change soon made in the manners of our inhabitants. From being thoughtless or indifferent about religion, it seemed as if all the world were growing religious, so that one could not walk thro' the town in an evening without hearing psalms sung in different families of every street.[16]

In 1764, Benjamin Franklin wrote a letter George Whitefield, ending with the salutation:

Your frequently repeated Wishes and Prayers for my Eternal as well as temporal Happiness are very obliging. I can only thank you for them, and offer you mine in return.[17]

In 1769, George Whitefield wrote to Benjamin Franklin on the night before his last trip to America. In this last surviving letter, Whitefield shared his desire that both he and Franklin would:

Be in that happy number of those who, in the midst of the tremendous final blaze, shall cry Amen.[18]

In the last letter Benjamin Franklin wrote to George Whitefield, he expressed:

Life, like a dramatic piece, should...finish handsomely. Being now in the last act, I began to cast about for something fit to end with...
I sometimes wish, that you and I were jointly employ'd by the Crown to settle a colony on the Ohio...to settle in that fine country a strong body of religious and industrious people!...
Might it not greatly facilitate the introduction of pure religion among the heathen, if we could, by such a colony, show them a better sample of Christians than they commonly see in our Indian traders?[19]

Almost never is Franklin portrayed in this light, and yet it was his heart's passion to see people come to Christ and have a Christian community where the examples of Christian living abound. Franklin's communication with revivalist Whitfield was characterized by his zeal and unashamedness when declaring the faith of the new nation.

In July of 1776, Benjamin Franklin was appointed part of a committee to draft a seal for the newly formed United States that would characterize the spirit of this new nation. He proposed:

Moses lifting up his wand, and dividing the red sea, and Pharaoh in his chariot overwhelmed with the waters. This motto: "Rebellion to tyrants is obedience to God. [20]

One of our most revered public symbols, the Liberty Bell, was founded in the biblical premise of celebrating a God-ordained season of blessing.

The Liberty Bell (August 1752), was cast in England by an order of the Pennsylvania Assembly to commemorate the fiftieth anniversary of the colony's existence. Founded in 1701, when William Penn wrote the Charter of Privileges, the colony's Assembly declared a "Year of Jubilee" in 1751, and commissioned a bell to be put in the Philadelphia State House.

The Liberty Bell received its name from being rung at the first public reading of the Declaration of Independence, July 8, 1776, and it cracked as it was rung at the funeral for Chief Justice John Marshall, 1835.

To cite its significance, Isaac Norris, the Speaker of the Pennsylvania Assembly, chose Leviticus chapter 25 verse 10:

And ye shall make hallow the fiftieth year, and proclaim liberty throughout all the land unto all the inhabitants thereof; it shall be a jubilee. [21]

The inscription cast onto the bell, August 1752, stated:

Proclaim liberty through all the land and to all the inhabitants thereof. (Leviticus XXV. 10) [22]

It is time we as a nation return to the concept of liberty which is even greater than freedom, for freedom indicates a legal position while liberty declares a spiritual condition recognizing the presence of the Lord. **"And where the Spirit of the Lord is, there is liberty." II Corinthians 3:17**

In a letter dated April 17, 1787, Benjamin Franklin stated:

Only a virtuous people are capable of freedom. As nations become corrupt and vicious, they have more need of masters.[23]

Small wonder, then, that our legislators continue to pile on law after law (while so much of what is already on the books is unenforced); that our courts continue to delve and interpret as an attempt to clarify intent—because an unprincipled and increasingly immoral nation is, according to a Founding Father, incapable of freedom, and therefore in need of more masters. Deep-seated moral and religious convictions provides a mastery of self that is dependent on the one true master, the Lord Jesus Christ, and other masters, such as the law, are less necessary.

Benjamin Franklin, even in the heyday of the new found faith-based experiment of self-government, expressed his concern that a lack of dependence on God would threaten the existence and success of independence politically and socially:

To that kind Providence we owe this happy opportunity of consulting in peace on the means of establishing our future national felicity. And have we now forgotten that powerful Friend? Or do we imagine we no longer need His assistance?

I have lived, Sir, a long time, and the longer I live, the more convincing proofs I see of this truth - that God Governs in the affairs of men. And if a sparrow cannot fall to the ground without His notice, is it probable that an empire can rise without His aid?

We have been assured, Sir, in the Sacred Writings, that "except the Lord build the House, they labor in vain that build it." I firmly believe this; and I also believe that without his concurring aid we shall succeed in this political building no better than the Builders of Babel: We shall be divided by our partial local interests; our projects will be confounded, and we ourselves shall become a reproach and bye word down to future ages.

And what is worse, mankind may hereafter from this unfortunate instance, despair of establishing Governments by Human wisdom and leave it to chance, war and conquest.

I therefore beg leave to move - that henceforth prayers imploring the assistance of Heaven, and its blessing on our deliberations, be held in this Assembly every morning before we proceed to business, and that one or more of the clergy of this city be requested to officiate in that service. [24]

On July 4th, the entire Convention assembled in the Reformed Calvinistic Lutheran Church, according to the proposal by Edmund Jennings Randolph of Virginia, and heard a sermon by Rev. William Rogers. His prayer reflected the hearts of the delegates following Franklin's admonition:

We fervently recommend to the fatherly notice...our federal convention...Favor them, from day to day, with thy inspiring presence; be their wisdom and strength; enable them to devise such measures as may prove happy instruments in healing all divisions and prove the good of the great whole;...that the United States of America may form one example of a free and virtuous government...

May we...continue, under the influence of republican virtue, to partake of all the blessings of cultivated and Christian society.[25]

Benjamin Franklin is attributed to have stated in a letter to the French ministry, March 1778:

Whoever shall introduce into public affairs the principles of primitive Christianity will change the face of the world.[26]

The experiment that those Founding Fathers undertook, with great humility and prayerfulness, has indeed changed the world we live in, and continues to do so. The personal challenge is for each one of us to revisit:
1) **The Faith,**
2) **The Responsibility to Community,**
3) **True Justice,**
4) **Courage,**
5) **Industry and Work Ethic,**
6) **Education of Character and Abilities,**
7) **And Spiritual Revival**

by which our Founding Fathers envisioned we continue to change the face of the world!

May God Bless America!

---

[1] Johnson, Edward. Edward Johnson, The Wonder-Working Providences of Sion's Saviour in New England, J. Franklin Jameson, ed., (pub. 1653; Barnes & Noble edition), p. 163. The Annals of America, 20 vols. (Chicago, IL: Encyclopedia Britannica, 1968), Vol. 1, p. 217-20.

[2] Winthrop, John. Peter Marshall and David Manuel, The Light and the Glory (Old Tappan, NJ: Fleming H. Revell Company, 1977), p. 148.

[3] Mather, Cotton. 1702. Cotton Mather, Magnalia Christi Americana, (The Great Achievement of Christ in America), 2 vols. (Edinburgh: The Banner of Truth Trust, 1702, 1979), 1:26. Gary DeMar, America's Christian History: The Untold Story (Atlanta, GA: American Vision Publishers, Inc., 1993), p. 47.

[4] Mather, Cotton. Cotton Mather, Magnalia Christi Americana. Stephen Foster, Their Solitary Way (New Haven: Yale University Press, 1971) p. 121. Peter Marshall and David Manuel, The Glory of America (Bloomington, MN: Garborg's Heart'N Home, Inc., 1991), 2.14.

[5] Pennsylvania, Frame of Government of. April 25, 1682, in the preface of his Frame of Government of Pennsylvania. A Collection of Charters and Other Public Acts Relating to the Province of Pennsylvania (Philadelphia: B. Franklin, 1740), pp. 10-12. Thomas Clarkson, Memoirs of the Private and Public Life of William Penn (London: Longman, Hurst, Orme, & Grown, 1813; Richard Taylor and Co., 1813), Vol. I, pp. 299-305. William Wistar Comfort, William Penn and Our Liberties (Published in the Penn Mutual's Centennial Year in honor of the man whose name the company adopted at its founding in the year 1847.) Philadelphia: The Penn Mutual Life Insurance Company, 1947, n.p. Benjamin Franklin Morris, The Christian Life and Character of the Civil Institutions of the United States (Philadelphia: George W. Childs, 1864), pp. 82-83. Frances Newton Thorpe, ed., Federal and State Constitutions, Colonial Charters, and Other Organic Laws of the States, Territories, and Colonies now or heretofore forming the United States, 7 vols. (Washington: Government Printing Office, 1905; 1909; St. Clair Shores, MI: Scholarly Press, 1968), Vol. V, pp. 3052-3059. Charles E. Rice, The Supreme Court and Public Prayer (New York: Fordham University Press, 1964), pp. 163-164. The Annals of America, 20 vols. (Chicago, IL: Encyclopedia Britannica, 1968), Vol. I, pp. 265-267. Richard L. Perry, ed., Sources of Our Liberties - Documentary Origins of Individual Liberties in the United States Constitution and Bill of Rights (Chicago: American Bar Foundation, 1978; New York: 1952). Gary DeMar, God and Government - A Biblical and Historical Study (Atlanta, GA: American Vision Press, 1982), p. 115. Stephen McDowell and Mark Beliles, "The Providential Perspective" (Charlottesville, VA: The Providence Foundation, P.O. Box 6759, Charlottesville, Va. 22906, January 1994), Vol. 9, No. 1, p. 1.

[6] Montesquieu, Baron Charles Louis Joseph de Secondat. Donald S. Lutz and Charles S. Hyneman, "The Relative Influence of European Writers on Late Eighteenth-Century American Political Thought," American Political Review 189 (1984): 189-197. (Courtesy of Dr. Wayne House of Dallas Theological Seminary.) John Eidsmoe, Christianity and the Constitution - The Faith of Our Founding Fathers (Grand Rapids, MI: Baker Book House, A Mott Media Book, 1987, 6th printing 1993), pp. 51-53. Stephen K. McDowell and Mark A. Beliles, America's Providential History (Charlottesville, VA: Providence Press, 1988), p. 156.

[7] Montesquieu, Baron Charles Louis Joseph de Secondat. 1748. The Spirit of the Laws (New York: Hafner, 1949, 1962), 1:1-3. John Eidsmoe, Christianity and the Constitution - The Faith of Our Founding Fathers (Grand Rapids, MI: Baker Book House, A Mott Media Book, 1987, 6th printing 1993), pp. 54-55.

[8] Montesquieu, Baron Charles Louis Joseph de Secondat. 1748. Baron Charles Montesquieu, The Spirit of the Laws, 1748, Anne Cohler, trans. (reprinted Cambridge: Cambridge University Press, 1989), p. 457.

[9] Montesquieu, Baron Charles Louis Joseph de Secondat. 1748. Baron Charles Montesquieu, The Spirit of the Laws, 1748, Anne Cohler, trans. (reprinted Cambridge: Cambridge University Press, 1989), p. 457.

[10] Montesquieu, Baron Charles Louis Joseph de Secondat. 1748. Baron Charles Montesquieu, The Spirit of the Laws, 1748, Anne Cohler, trans. (reprinted Cambridge: Cambridge University Press, 1989), p. 457.

[11] Montesquieu, Baron Charles Louis Joseph de Secondat. 1748. Baron Charles Montesquieu, The Spirit of the Laws, 1748, Anne Cohler, trans. (reprinted Cambridge: Cambridge University Press, 1989), p. 157.

[12] Edwards, Jonathan. The Works of President Edwards (Isaiah Thomas, ed.), pp. 14-19. Peter Marshall and David Manuel, The Light and The Glory (Old Tappan, NJ: Fleming H. Revell Company), pp. 241-243.

[13] Montesquieu, Baron Charles Louis Joseph de Secondat. 1748. The Spirit of the Laws (New York: Hafner, 1949, 1962), 24:27-29. John Eidsmoe, Christianity and the Constitution - The Faith of Our Founding Fathers (Grand Rapids, MI: Baker Book House, A Mott Media Book, 1987, 6th printing 1993), pp. 55-56. Stephen Abbott Northrop, D.D., A Cloud of Witnesses (Portland, OR: American Heritage Ministries, 1987; Mantle Ministries, 228 Still Ridge, Bulverde, Texas), p. 322.

[14] Franklin, Benjamin. 1754. Benjamin Franklin, Information on Those Who Would Remove to America (London: M. Gurney, 1754), pp. 22, 23. "Advice on Coming to America," George D. Youstra, ed., America in Person (Greenville, SC: Bob Jones University Press, 1975), p. 109. Tim LaHaye, Faith of Our Founding Fathers (Brentwood, TN: Wolgemuth & Hyatt, Publishers, Inc. 1987), p. 31. Benjamin Franklin, Works of the Late Doctor Benjamin Franklin Consisting of His Life, Written by Himself, Together with Essays, Humorous, Moral & Literary, Chiefly in the Manner of the Spectator, Richard Price, ed., (Dublin: P. Wogan, P. Byrne, J. Moore, and W. Jones, 1793), p. 289.

[15] Trumbull, Jonathan. April 19, 1775, as Governor of the Connecticut Colony proclaiming a day of fasting and prayer. Verna M. Hall, The Christian History of the American Revolution (San Francisco: Foundation for American Christian Education, 1976), p. 407. Peter Marshall and David Manuel, The Glory of America (Bloomington, MN: Garborg's Heart'N Home, Inc., 1991), 3.22. Marshall Foster and Mary-Elaine Swanson, The American Covenant - The Untold Story (Roseburg, OR: Foundation for Christian Self-Government, 1981; Thousand Oaks, CA: The Mayflower Institute, 1983, 1992), p. 120.

[16] Franklin, Benjamin. 1739. Benjamin Franklin, The Autobiography of Benjamin Franklin (New York: Books,Inc., 1791), p. 146. Benjamin Franklin, Autobiography, 1771-75 (Reprinted Garden City, NY: Garden City Publishing Co., Inc., 1916), Vol. 1, pp. 191-192. John Pollack, George Whitefield and the Great Awakening (Garden City New Jersey: Doubleday and Co., 1972), p. 117.

John Eidsmoe, Christianity and The Constitution - The Faith of Our Founding Fathers (Grand Rapids, MI: Baker Book House, 1987), p. 204. Tim LaHaye, Faith of Our Founding Fathers (Brentwood, TN: Wolgemuth & Hyatt, Publishers, Inc., 1987), p. 116. Peter Marshall & David Manuel, The Glory of America (Bloomington, MN: Garborg's Heart 'N Home, 1991), 12.18.

[17] Franklin, Benjamin. 1764, in ending a letter written to George Whitefield. Frank Lambert, The Religious Odd Couple (Carol Stream, IL: Christian History), Vol. XII, No. 2, Issue 38, p. 31

[18] Franklin, Benjamin. 1769, in the last surviving letter from George Whitefield to Benjamin Franklin. Frank Lambert, The Religious Odd Couple (Carol Stream, IL: Christian History), Vol. XII, No. 2, Issue 38, pp. 31-32.

[19] Franklin, Benjamin. In his last letter to George Whitefield. Frank Lambert, The Religious Odd Couple (Carol Stream, IL: Christian History), Vol. XII, No. 2, Issue 38, p. 31.

[20] Franklin, Benjamin. August 14, 1776. Charles Francis Adams (son of John Quincy Adams and grandson of John Adams), ed., Letters of John Adams, Addressed to His Wife, (Boston: Charles C. Little and James Brown, 1841), Vol. I, p. 152. L.H. Butterfield, Marc Frielander and Mary-Jo Kings, eds. The Book of Abigail and John - Selected Letters from The Adams Family 1762-1784 (Cambridge, MA: Harvard University Press, 1975), p. 154.

[21] Liberty Bell. Committee on the Restoration of Independence Hall, Mayor's Office. Report. Philadelphia, June 12, 1873. Library of Congress Rare Book Collection, Washington, D.C., pp. 2-3.

[22] Liberty Bell. "Our Christian Heritage," Letter from Plymouth Rock (Marlborough, NH: The Plymouth Rock Foundation), p. 2. D.P. Diffine, Ph.D., One Nation Under God - How Close a Separation? (Searcy, Arkansas: Harding University, Belden Center for Private Enterprise Education, 6th edition, 1992), p. 5.

[23] . Franklin, Benjamin. April 17, 1787, in a letter. Albert Henry Smyth, ed., The Writings of Benjamin Franklin, 10 vols. (New York: Macmillan Co., 1905-7), 9:569, reprinted (NY: Haskell House Publishers, 1970), Vol. IX, p. 569. Albert Henry Smyth, ed., The Writings of Benjamin Franklin 10 vols. (NY: The Macmillan Co., 1905-07), Vol. X, p. 50. Norman Cousins, In God We Trust - The Religious Beliefs and Ideas of the American Founding Fathers (NY: Harper & Brothers, Publishers, 1955), p. 393. Andrew W. Allison, Cleon Skousen and M. Richard Maxfield, The Real Benjamin Franklin (Salt Lake City, Utah: The Freeman Institute, 1982), p. 313. John Eidsmoe, Christianity and The Constitution - The Faith of Our Founding Fathers (Grand Rapids, MI: Baker Book House, 1987), p. 211. Tim LaHaye, Faith of Our Founding Fathers (Brentwood, TN: Wolgemuth & Hyatt, Publishers, Inc., 1987), p. 196. Stephen McDowell and Mark Beliles, "The Providential Perspective" (Charlottesville, VA: The Providence Foundation, P.O. Box 6759, Charlottesville, Va. 22906, January 1994), Vol. 9, No. 1, p. 4.

[24] Franklin, Benjamin. June 28, 1787. James Madison, Notes of Debates in the Federal Convention of 1787 (NY: W.W. Morton & Co., Original 1787 reprinted 1987), Vol. I, p. 504, 451-21. James Madison, Notes of Debates in the Federal Convention of 1787 (Athens, Ohio: Ohio University Press, 1966, 1985), pp. 209-10. Henry D. Gilpin, editor, The Papers of James Madison

(Washington: Langtree & O' Sullivan, 1840), Vol. II, p. 985. George Bancroft, Bancroft's History of the Constitution of the United States vols. I-X (Boston: Charles C. Little & James Brown, 1838), Vol. II. Albert Henry Smyth, ed., The Writings of Benjamin Franklin (New York: The Macmillan Company, 1905-7), Vol. IX, pp. 600-601. Gaillard Hunt and James B. Scott, ed., The Debates in the Federal Convention of 1787 Which Framed the Constitution of the United States of America, reported by James Madison (New York: Oxford University Press, 1920), pp. 181-182. Andrew M. Allison, W. Cleon Skousen, and M. Richard Maxfield, The Real Benjamin Franklin (Salt Lake City, Utah: The Freeman Institute, 1982, pp. 258-259. John Eidsmoe, Christianity and the Constitution - The Faith of Our Founding Fathers (Grand Rapids, MI: Baker Book House, A Mott Media Book, 1987, 6th printing 1993), pp. 12-13, 208. Tim LaHaye, Faith of Our Founding Fathers (Brentwood, TN: Wolgemuth & Hyatt, Publishers, Inc., 1987), pp. 122-124. Stephen Abbott Northrop, D.D., A Cloud of Witnesses (Portland, Oregon: American Heritage Ministries, 1987; Mantle Ministries, 228 Still Ridge, Bulverde, Texas), p. 159-160. D.P. Diffine, Ph.D., One Nation Under God - How Close a Separation? (Searcy, Arkansas: Harding University, Belden Center for Private Enterprise Education, 6th edition, 1992), p. 8. Stephen McDowell and Mark Beliles, "The Providential Perspective" (Charlottesville, VA: The Providence Foundation, P.O. Box 6759, Charlottesville, Va. 22906, January 1994), Vol. 9, No. 1, pp. 5-6.

[25] Franklin, Benjamin. Benjamin Franklin Morris, The Christian Life and Character of the Civil Institutions of the United States (Philadelphia: George W. Childs, 1864), pp. 253-254.

[26] Franklin, Benjamin. Attributed, March 1778, in a letter to the French ministry. Charles E. Kistler, This Nation Under God (Boston: Richard G. Badger, The Gorham Press, 1924), p. 83. Burton Stevenson, The Home Book of Quotations-Classical & Modern (New York: Dodd, Mead and Company, 1967), pp. 151, 265. Peter Marshall and David Manuel, The Light and the Glory (NJ: Fleming H. Revell Co., 1977; 1986), p. 370, n. 10. D.P. Diffine, Ph.D., One Nation Under God - How Close a Separation? (Searcy, Arkansas: Harding University, Belden Center for Private Enterprise Education, 6th edition, 1992), p. 9. Sam Bartholomew, God's Role in America (Nashville, TN: Eggman Publishing Company, 1996), p. 39. Matthew Staver, Faith and Freedom (Wheaton, IL: Crossway Books, 1995), p. 18.

For more information, speaking engagements, and additional resources contact NAME:

The National Association of Marriage Enhancement
P. O. Box 30777
Phoenix, Arizona U.S.A.
85046-0777

602-404-2600
602-971-7127 fax
or
www.nameonline.net

Other Books by Leo Godzich
Is God In Your Marriage?
Mighty Men
Couple-to-Couple Scripture Reference Guide
Public Relations & The Church
Is God In Your Marriage? Curriculum & Study Guide
Together Again: Inspiring Marriage Restorations (June 2002)
Men Are From Dirt, Women Are From Men (September 2002)